AFRIKAANS

VOCABULARY

ENGLISH-AFRIKAANS

The most useful words
To expand your lexicon and sharpen
your language skills

3000 words

Afrikaans vocabulary for English speakers - 3000 words

By Andrey Taranov

T&P Books vocabularies are intended for helping you learn, memorize and review foreign words. The dictionary is divided into themes, covering all major spheres of everyday activities, business, science, culture, etc.

The process of learning words using T&P Books' theme-based dictionaries gives you the following advantages:

- Correctly grouped source information predetermines success at subsequent stages of word memorization
- Availability of words derived from the same root allowing memorization of word units (rather than separate words)
- Small units of words facilitate the process of establishing associative links needed for consolidation of vocabulary
- Level of language knowledge can be estimated by the number of learned words

T&P Books Publishing
www.tpbooks.com

ISBN: 978-1-78716-486-4

This book is also available in E-book formats.
Please visit www.tpbooks.com or the major online bookstores.

AFRIKAANS VOCABULARY
for English speakers

T&P Books vocabularies are intended to help you learn, memorize, and review foreign words. The vocabulary contains over 3000 commonly used words arranged thematically.

- Vocabulary contains the most commonly used words
- Recommended as an addition to any language course
- Meets the needs of beginners and advanced learners of foreign languages
- Convenient for daily use, revision sessions, and self-testing activities
- Allows you to assess your vocabulary

Special features of the vocabulary

- Words are organized according to their meaning, not alphabetically
- Words are presented in three columns to facilitate the reviewing and self-testing processes
- Words in groups are divided into small blocks to facilitate the learning process
- The vocabulary offers a convenient and simple transcription of each foreign word

The vocabulary has 101 topics including:

Basic Concepts, Numbers, Colors, Months, Seasons, Units of Measurement, Clothing & Accessories, Food & Nutrition, Restaurant, Family Members, Relatives, Character, Feelings, Emotions, Diseases, City, Town, Sightseeing, Shopping, Money, House, Home, Office, Working in the Office, Import & Export, Marketing, Job Search, Sports, Education, Computer, Internet, Tools, Nature, Countries, Nationalities and more ...

T&P BOOKS' THEME-BASED DICTIONARIES

The Correct System for Memorizing Foreign Words

Acquiring vocabulary is one of the most important elements of learning a foreign language, because words allow us to express our thoughts, ask questions, and provide answers. An inadequate vocabulary can impede communication with a foreigner and make it difficult to understand a book or movie well.

The pace of activity in all spheres of modern life, including the learning of modern languages, has increased. Today, we need to memorize large amounts of information (grammar rules, foreign words, etc.) within a short period. However, this does not need to be difficult. All you need to do is to choose the right training materials, learn a few special techniques, and develop your individual training system.

Having a system is critical to the process of language learning. Many people fail to succeed in this regard; they cannot master a foreign language because they fail to follow a system comprised of selecting materials, organizing lessons, arranging new words to be learned, and so on. The lack of a system causes confusion and eventually, lowers self-confidence.

T&P Books' theme-based dictionaries can be included in the list of elements needed for creating an effective system for learning foreign words. These dictionaries were specially developed for learning purposes and are meant to help students effectively memorize words and expand their vocabulary.

Generally speaking, the process of learning words consists of three main elements:

- Reception (creation or acquisition) of a training material, such as a word list
- Work aimed at memorizing new words
- Work aimed at reviewing the learned words, such as self-testing

All three elements are equally important since they determine the quality of work and the final result. All three processes require certain skills and a well-thought-out approach.

New words are often encountered quite randomly when learning a foreign language and it may be difficult to include them all in a unified list. As a result, these words remain written on scraps of paper, in book margins, textbooks, and so on. In order to systematize such words, we have to create and continually update a "book of new words." A paper notebook, a netbook, or a tablet PC can be used for these purposes.

This "book of new words" will be your personal, unique list of words. However, it will only contain the words that you came across during the learning process. For example, you might have written down the words "Sunday," "Tuesday," and "Friday." However, there are additional words for days of the week, for example, "Saturday," that are missing, and your list of words would be incomplete. Using a theme dictionary, in addition to the "book of new words," is a reasonable solution to this problem.

The theme-based dictionary may serve as the basis for expanding your vocabulary.

It will be your big "book of new words" containing the most frequently used words of a foreign language already included. There are quite a few theme-based dictionaries available, and you should ensure that you make the right choice in order to get the maximum benefit from your purchase.

Therefore, we suggest using theme-based dictionaries from T&P Books Publishing as an aid to learning foreign words. Our books are specially developed for effective use in the sphere of vocabulary systematization, expansion and review.

Theme-based dictionaries are not a magical solution to learning new words. However, they can serve as your main database to aid foreign-language acquisition. Apart from theme dictionaries, you can have copybooks for writing down new words, flash cards, glossaries for various texts, as well as other resources; however, a good theme dictionary will always remain your primary collection of words.

T&P Books' theme-based dictionaries are specialty books that contain the most frequently used words in a language.

The main characteristic of such dictionaries is the division of words into themes. For example, the *City* theme contains the words "street," "crossroads," "square," "fountain," and so on. The *Talking* theme might contain words like "to talk," "to ask," "question," and "answer".

All the words in a theme are divided into smaller units, each comprising 3–5 words. Such an arrangement improves the perception of words and makes the learning process less tiresome. Each unit contains a selection of words with similar meanings or identical roots. This allows you to learn words in small groups and establish other associative links that have a positive effect on memorization.

The words on each page are placed in three columns: a word in your native language, its translation, and its transcription. Such positioning allows for the use of techniques for effective memorization. After closing the translation column, you can flip through and review foreign words, and vice versa. "This is an easy and convenient method of review – one that we recommend you do often."

Our theme-based dictionaries contain transcriptions for all the foreign words. Unfortunately, none of the existing transcriptions are able to convey the exact nuances of foreign pronunciation. That is why we recommend using the transcriptions only as a supplementary learning aid. Correct pronunciation can only be acquired with the help of sound. Therefore our collection includes audio theme-based dictionaries.

The process of learning words using T&P Books' theme-based dictionaries gives you the following advantages:

- You have correctly grouped source information, which predetermines your success at subsequent stages of word memorization
- Availability of words derived from the same root (lazy, lazily, lazybones), allowing you to memorize word units instead of separate words
- Small units of words facilitate the process of establishing associative links needed for consolidation of vocabulary
- You can estimate the number of learned words and hence your level of language knowledge
- The dictionary allows for the creation of an effective and high-quality revision process
- You can revise certain themes several times, modifying the revision methods and techniques
- Audio versions of the dictionaries help you to work out the pronunciation of words and develop your skills of auditory word perception

The T&P Books' theme-based dictionaries are offered in several variants differing in the number of words: 1.500, 3.000, 5.000, 7.000, and 9.000 words. There are also dictionaries containing 15,000 words for some language combinations. Your choice of dictionary will depend on your knowledge level and goals.

We sincerely believe that our dictionaries will become your trusty assistant in learning foreign languages and will allow you to easily acquire the necessary vocabulary.

TABLE OF CONTENTS

PRONUNCIATION GUIDE

T&P phonetic alphabet	Afrikaans example	English example
[a]	land	shorter than in ask
[ā]	straat	calf, palm
[æ]	hout	chess, man
[o], [ɔ]	Australië	drop, baught
[e]	metaal	elm, medal
[ɛ]	aanlê	man, bad
[ə]	filter	driver, teacher
[ɪ]	uur	big, America
[i]	billik	shorter than in feet
[ī]	naïef	tree, big
[o]	koppie	pod, John
[ø]	akteur	eternal, church
[œ]	fluit	German Hölle
[u]	hulle	book
[ʊ]	hout	good, booklet
[b]	bakker	baby, book
[d]	donder	day, doctor
[f]	navraag	face, food
[g]	burger	game, gold
[h]	driehoek	home, have
[j]	byvoeg	yes, New York
[k]	kamera	clock, kiss
[l]	loon	lace, people
[m]	môre	magic, milk
[n]	neef	sang, thing
[p]	pyp	pencil, private
[r]	rigting	rice, radio
[s]	oplos	city, boss
[t]	lood, tenk	tourist, trip
[v]	bewaar	very, river
[w]	oorwinnaar	vase, winter
[z]	zoem	zebra, please
[dʒ]	enjin	joke, general
[ʃ]	artisjok	machine, shark
[ŋ]	kans	English, ring

T&P phonetic alphabet	Afrikaans example	English example
[ʧ]	tjek	church, French
[ʒ]	beige	forge, pleasure
[x]	agent	as in Scots 'loch'

ABBREVIATIONS
used in the vocabulary

English abbreviations

ab.	-	about
adj	-	adjective
adv	-	adverb
anim.	-	animate
as adj	-	attributive noun used as adjective
e.g.	-	for example
etc.	-	et cetera
fam.	-	familiar
fem.	-	feminine
form.	-	formal
inanim.	-	inanimate
masc.	-	masculine
math	-	mathematics
mil.	-	military
n	-	noun
pl	-	plural
pron.	-	pronoun
sb	-	somebody
sing.	-	singular
sth	-	something
v aux	-	auxiliary verb
vi	-	intransitive verb
vi, vt	-	intransitive, transitive verb
vt	-	transitive verb

BASIC CONCEPTS

1. Pronouns

I, me	**ek, my**	[ɛk], [maj]
you	**jy**	[jaj]
he	**hy**	[haj]
she	**sy**	[saj]
it	**dit**	[dit]
we	**ons**	[ɔŋs]
you (to a group)	**julle**	[jullə]
you (polite, sing.)	**u**	[u]
you (polite, pl)	**u**	[u]
they	**hulle**	[hullə]

2. Greetings. Salutations

Hello! (fam.)	**Hallo!**	[hallo!]
Hello! (form.)	**Hallo!**	[hallo!]
Good morning!	**Goeie môre!**	[χuje mɔrə!]
Good afternoon!	**Goeiemiddag!**	[χuje·middaχ!]
Good evening!	**Goeienaand!**	[χuje·nãnt!]
to say hello	**dagsê**	[daχsɛ:]
Hi! (hello)	**Hallo!**	[hallo!]
greeting (n)	**groet**	[χrut]
to greet (vt)	**groet**	[χrut]
How are you?	**Hoe gaan dit?**	[hu χãn dit?]
What's new?	**Hoe gaan dit?**	[hu χãn dit?]
Goodbye!	**Totsiens!**	[totsiŋs!]
Bye!	**Koebaai!**	[kubãi!]
See you soon!	**Totsiens!**	[totsiŋs!]
Farewell!	**Totsiens!**	[totsiŋs!]
Farewell! (to a friend)	**Mooi loop!**	[moj loəp!]
Farewell! (form.)	**Vaarwel!**	[fãrwell!]
to say goodbye	**afskeid neem**	[afskæjt neəm]
So long!	**Koebaai!**	[kubãi!]
Thank you!	**Dankie!**	[danki!]
Thank you very much!	**Baie dankie!**	[baje danki!]
You're welcome	**Plesier**	[plesir]

| Don't mention it! | **Plesier!** | [plesir!] |
| It was nothing | **Plesier** | [plesir] |

Excuse me! (fam.)	**Ekskuus!**	[ɛkskɪs!]
Excuse me! (form.)	**Verskoon my!**	[ferskoən maj!]
to excuse (forgive)	**verskoon**	[ferskoən]

to apologize (vi)	**verskoning vra**	[ferskoniŋ fra]
My apologies	**Verskoning**	[ferskoniŋ]
I'm sorry!	**Ek is jammer!**	[ɛk is jammər!]
to forgive (vt)	**vergewe**	[ferχevə]
It's okay! (that's all right)	**Maak nie saak nie!**	[mãk ni sãk ni!]
please (adv)	**asseblief**	[asseblif]

Don't forget!	**Vergeet dit nie!**	[ferχeət dit ni!]
Certainly!	**Beslis!**	[beslis!]
Of course not!	**Natuurlik nie!**	[natɪrlik ni!]
Okay! (I agree)	**OK!**	[okej!]
That's enough!	**Dis genoeg!**	[dis χenuχ!]

3. Questions

Who?	**Wie?**	[vi?]
What?	**Wat?**	[vat?]
Where? (at, in)	**Waar?**	[vār?]
Where (to)?	**Waarheen?**	[vārheən?]
From where?	**Waarvandaan?**	[vārfandān?]
When?	**Wanneer?**	[vanneər?]
Why? (What for?)	**Hoekom?**	[hukom?]
Why? (~ are you crying?)	**Hoekom?**	[hukom?]

What for?	**Vir wat?**	[fir vat?]
How? (in what way)	**Hoe?**	[hu?]
What? (What kind of …?)	**Watter?**	[vatter?]
Which?	**Watter een?**	[vatter eən?]

To whom?	**Vir wie?**	[fir vi?]
About whom?	**Oor wie?**	[oər vi?]
About what?	**Oor wat?**	[oər vat?]
With whom?	**Met wie?**	[met vi?]
How many? How much?	**Hoeveel?**	[hufeəl?]

4. Prepositions

with (accompanied by)	**met**	[met]
without	**sonder**	[sondər]
to (indicating direction)	**na**	[na]
about (talking ~ …)	**oor**	[oər]

before (in time)	**voor**	[foər]
in front of ...	**voor ...**	[foər ...]
under (beneath, below)	**onder**	[ondər]
above (over)	**oor**	[oər]
on (atop)	**op**	[op]
from (off, out of)	**uit**	[œit]
of (made from)	**van**	[fan]
in (e.g., ~ ten minutes)	**oor**	[oər]
over (across the top of)	**oor**	[oər]

5. Function words. Adverbs. Part 1

Where? (at, in)	**Waar?**	[vār?]
here (adv)	**hier**	[hir]
there (adv)	**daar**	[dār]
somewhere (to be)	**êrens**	[ærɛŋs]
nowhere (not anywhere)	**nêrens**	[nærɛŋs]
by (near, beside)	**by**	[baj]
by the window	**by**	[baj]
Where (to)?	**Waarheen?**	[vārheən?]
here (e.g., come ~!)	**hier**	[hir]
there (e.g., to go ~)	**soontoe**	[soentu]
from here (adv)	**hiervandaan**	[hirfandān]
from there (adv)	**daarvandaan**	[dārfandān]
close (adv)	**naby**	[nabaj]
far (adv)	**ver**	[fer]
near (e.g., ~ Paris)	**naby**	[nabaj]
nearby (adv)	**naby**	[nabaj]
not far (adv)	**nie ver nie**	[ni fər ni]
left (adj)	**linker-**	[linkər-]
on the left	**op linkerhand**	[op linkərhant]
to the left	**na links**	[na links]
right (adj)	**regter**	[reχtər]
on the right	**op regterhand**	[op reχtərhant]
to the right	**na regs**	[na reχs]
in front (adv)	**voor**	[foər]
front (as adj)	**voorste**	[foərstə]
ahead (the kids ran ~)	**vooruit**	[foərœit]
behind (adv)	**agter**	[aχtər]
from behind	**van agter**	[fan aχtər]

back (towards the rear)	**agtertoe**	[aχtərtu]
middle	**middel**	[middəl]
in the middle	**in die middel**	[in di middəl]

at the side	**op die sykant**	[op di sajkant]
everywhere (adv)	**orals**	[orals]
around (in all directions)	**orals rond**	[orals ront]

from inside	**van binne**	[fan binnə]
somewhere (to go)	**êrens**	[ærɛŋs]
straight (directly)	**reguit**	[reχœit]
back (e.g., come ~)	**terug**	[teruχ]

| from anywhere | **êrens vandaan** | [ærɛŋs fandãn] |
| from somewhere | **êrens vandaan** | [ærɛŋs fandãn] |

firstly (adv)	**in die eerste plek**	[in di eərstə plek]
secondly (adv)	**in die tweede plek**	[in di tweədə plek]
thirdly (adv)	**in die derde plek**	[in di derdə plek]

suddenly (adv)	**skielik**	[skilik]
at first (in the beginning)	**aan die begin**	[ãn di beχin]
for the first time	**vir die eerste keer**	[fir di eərstə keər]
long before …	**lank voordat …**	[lank foərdat …]
anew (over again)	**opnuut**	[opnɪt]
for good (adv)	**vir goed**	[fir χut]

never (adv)	**nooit**	[nojt]
again (adv)	**weer**	[veər]
now (adv)	**nou**	[næʊ]
often (adv)	**dikwels**	[dikwɛls]
then (adv)	**toe**	[tu]
urgently (quickly)	**dringend**	[driŋən]
usually (adv)	**gewoonlik**	[χevoənlik]

by the way, …	**terloops, …**	[terloəps], […]
possible (that is ~)	**moontlik**	[moəntlik]
probably (adv)	**waarskynlik**	[vãrskajnlik]
maybe (adv)	**dalk**	[dalk]
besides …	**trouens...**	[træʊɛŋs...]
that's why …	**dis hoekom …**	[dis hukom …]
in spite of …	**ondanks …**	[ondanks …]
thanks to …	**danksy …**	[danksaj …]

what (pron.)	**wat**	[vat]
that (conj.)	**dat**	[dat]
something	**iets**	[its]
anything (something)	**iets**	[its]
nothing	**niks**	[niks]

| who (pron.) | **wie** | [vi] |
| someone | **iemand** | [imant] |

somebody	iemand	[imant]
nobody	niemand	[nimant]
nowhere (a voyage to ~)	nêrens	[nærɛŋs]
nobody's	niemand se	[nimant sə]
somebody's	iemand se	[imant sə]

so (I'm ~ glad)	so	[so]
also (as well)	ook	[oək]
too (as well)	ook	[oək]

6. Function words. Adverbs. Part 2

| Why? | Waarom? | [vărom?] |
| because ... | omdat ... | [omdat ...] |

and	en	[ɛn]
or	of	[of]
but	maar	[mǎr]
for (e.g., ~ me)	vir	[fir]

too (~ many people)	te	[te]
only (exclusively)	net	[net]
exactly (adv)	presies	[presis]
about (more or less)	ongeveer	[onχəfeər]

approximately (adv)	ongeveer	[onχəfeər]
approximate (adj)	geraamde	[χerǎmdə]
almost (adv)	amper	[ampər]
the rest	die res	[di res]

the other (second)	die ander	[di andər]
other (different)	ander	[andər]
each (adj)	elke	[ɛlkə]
any (no matter which)	enige	[ɛniχə]
many (adv)	baie	[bajə]
much (adv)	baie	[bajə]
many people	baie mense	[bajə mɛŋsə]
all (everyone)	almal	[almal]

in return for ...	in ruil vir...	[in rœil fir...]
in exchange (adv)	as vergoeding	[as ferχudiŋ]
by hand (made)	met die hand	[met di hant]
hardly (negative opinion)	skaars	[skǎrs]

probably (adv)	waarskynlik	[vǎrskajnlik]
on purpose (intentionally)	opsetlik	[opsetlik]
by accident (adv)	toevallig	[tufalləχ]

| very (adv) | baie | [bajə] |
| for example (adv) | byvoorbeeld | [bajfoərbeəlt] |

between	**tussen**	[tussən]
among	**tussen**	[tussən]
so much (such a lot)	**so baie**	[so baje]
especially (adv)	**veral**	[feral]

NUMBERS. MISCELLANEOUS

7. Cardinal numbers. Part 1

0 zero	nul	[nul]
1 one	een	[eən]
2 two	twee	[tweə]
3 three	drie	[dri]
4 four	vier	[fir]
5 five	vyf	[fajf]
6 six	ses	[ses]
7 seven	sewe	[sevə]
8 eight	ag	[aχ]
9 nine	nege	[neχə]
10 ten	tien	[tin]
11 eleven	elf	[ɛlf]
12 twelve	twaalf	[twālf]
13 thirteen	dertien	[dertin]
14 fourteen	veertien	[feərtin]
15 fifteen	vyftien	[fajftin]
16 sixteen	sestien	[sestin]
17 seventeen	sewetien	[sevətin]
18 eighteen	agtien	[aχtin]
19 nineteen	negetien	[neχetin]
20 twenty	twintig	[twintəχ]
21 twenty-one	een-en-twintig	[eən-en-twintəχ]
22 twenty-two	twee-en-twintig	[tweə-en-twintəχ]
23 twenty-three	drie-en-twintig	[dri-en-twintəχ]
30 thirty	dertig	[dertəχ]
31 thirty-one	een-en-dertig	[eən-en-dertəχ]
32 thirty-two	twee-en-dertig	[tweə-en-dertəχ]
33 thirty-three	drie-en-dertig	[dri-en-dertəχ]
40 forty	veertig	[feərtəχ]
41 forty-one	een-en-veertig	[eən-en-feərtəχ]
42 forty-two	twee-en-veertig	[tweə-en-feərtəχ]
43 forty-three	vier-en-veertig	[fir-en-feərtəχ]
50 fifty	vyftig	[fajftəχ]
51 fifty-one	een-en-vyftig	[eən-en-fajftəχ]
52 fifty-two	twee-en-vyftig	[tweə-en-fajftəχ]

53 fifty-three	drie-en-vyftig	[dri-en-fajftəχ]
60 sixty	sestig	[sestəχ]
61 sixty-one	een-en-sestig	[eən-en-sestəχ]
62 sixty-two	twee-en-sestig	[tweə-en-sestəχ]
63 sixty-three	drie-en-sestig	[dri-en-sestəχ]
70 seventy	sewentig	[seventəχ]
71 seventy-one	een-en-sewentig	[eən-en-seventəχ]
72 seventy-two	twee-en-sewentig	[tweə-en-seventəχ]
73 seventy-three	drie-en-sewentig	[dri-en-seventəχ]
80 eighty	tagtig	[taχtəχ]
81 eighty-one	een-en-tagtig	[eən-en-taχtəχ]
82 eighty-two	twee-en-tagtig	[tweə-en-taχtəχ]
83 eighty-three	drie-en-tagtig	[dri-en-taχtəχ]
90 ninety	negentig	[neχentəχ]
91 ninety-one	een-en-negentig	[eən-en-neχentəχ]
92 ninety-two	twee-en-negentig	[tweə-en-neχentəχ]
93 ninety-three	drie-en-negentig	[dri-en-neχentəχ]

8. Cardinal numbers. Part 2

100 one hundred	honderd	[hondərt]
200 two hundred	tweehonderd	[tweə·hondərt]
300 three hundred	driehonderd	[dri·hondərt]
400 four hundred	vierhonderd	[fir·hondərt]
500 five hundred	vyfhonderd	[fajf·hondərt]
600 six hundred	seshonderd	[ses·hondərt]
700 seven hundred	sewehonderd	[sevə·hondərt]
800 eight hundred	aghonderd	[aχ·hondərt]
900 nine hundred	negehonderd	[neχə·hondərt]
1000 one thousand	duisend	[dœisent]
2000 two thousand	tweeduisend	[tweə·dœisent]
3000 three thousand	drieduisend	[dri·dœisent]
10000 ten thousand	tienduisend	[tin·dœisent]
one hundred thousand	honderdduisend	[hondərt·dajsent]
million	miljoen	[miljun]
billion	miljard	[miljart]

9. Ordinal numbers

first (adj)	eerste	[eərstə]
second (adj)	tweede	[tweedə]
third (adj)	derde	[derdə]
fourth (adj)	vierde	[firdə]

fifth (adj)	**vyfde**	[fajfdə]
sixth (adj)	**sesde**	[sesdə]
seventh (adj)	**sewende**	[sevendə]
eighth (adj)	**agste**	[aχstə]
ninth (adj)	**negende**	[neχendə]
tenth (adj)	**tiende**	[tində]

COLOURS. UNITS OF MEASUREMENT

10. Colors

color	**kleur**	[kløər]
shade (tint)	**skakering**	[skakeriŋ]
hue	**tint**	[tint]
rainbow	**reënboog**	[reɛn·boəχ]
white (adj)	**wit**	[vit]
black (adj)	**swart**	[swart]
gray (adj)	**grys**	[χrajs]
green (adj)	**groen**	[χrun]
yellow (adj)	**geel**	[χeəl]
red (adj)	**rooi**	[roj]
blue (adj)	**blou**	[blæʊ]
light blue (adj)	**ligblou**	[liχ·blæʊ]
pink (adj)	**pienk**	[pink]
orange (adj)	**oranje**	[oranje]
violet (adj)	**pers**	[pers]
brown (adj)	**bruin**	[brœin]
golden (adj)	**goue**	[χæʊə]
silvery (adj)	**silweragtig**	[silweraχtəχ]
beige (adj)	**beige**	[bɛ:iʒ]
cream (adj)	**roomkleurig**	[roəm·kløərəχ]
turquoise (adj)	**turkoois**	[turkojs]
cherry red (adj)	**kersierooi**	[kersi·roj]
lilac (adj)	**lila**	[lila]
crimson (adj)	**karmosyn**	[karmosajn]
light (adj)	**lig**	[liχ]
dark (adj)	**donker**	[donkər]
bright, vivid (adj)	**helder**	[hɛldər]
colored (pencils)	**kleurig**	[kløərəχ]
color (e.g., ~ film)	**kleur**	[kløər]
black-and-white (adj)	**swart-wit**	[swart-wit]
plain (one-colored)	**effe**	[ɛffə]
multicolored (adj)	**veelkleurig**	[feəlkløərəχ]

11. Units of measurement

weight	**gewig**	[χevəχ]
length	**lengte**	[leŋtə]
width	**breedte**	[breədtə]
height	**hoogte**	[hoəχtə]
depth	**diepte**	[diptə]
volume	**volume**	[folumə]
area	**area**	[areə]
gram	**gram**	[χram]
milligram	**milligram**	[milliχram]
kilogram	**kilogram**	[kiloχram]
ton	**ton**	[ton]
pound	**pond**	[pont]
ounce	**ons**	[ɔŋs]
meter	**meter**	[metər]
millimeter	**millimeter**	[millimetər]
centimeter	**sentimeter**	[sentimetər]
kilometer	**kilometer**	[kilometər]
mile	**myl**	[majl]
inch	**duim**	[dœim]
foot	**voet**	[fut]
yard	**jaart**	[jãrt]
square meter	**vierkante meter**	[firkantə metər]
hectare	**hektaar**	[hektãr]
liter	**liter**	[litər]
degree	**graad**	[χrãt]
volt	**volt**	[folt]
ampere	**ampère**	[ampɛ:r]
horsepower	**perdekrag**	[perdə·kraχ]
quantity	**hoeveelheid**	[hufeəlhæjt]
half	**helfte**	[hɛlftə]
dozen	**dosyn**	[dosajn]
piece (item)	**stuk**	[stuk]
size	**grootte**	[χroəttə]
scale (map ~)	**skaal**	[skãl]
minimal (adj)	**minimaal**	[minimãl]
the smallest (adj)	**die kleinste**	[di klæjnstə]
medium (adj)	**medium**	[medium]
maximal (adj)	**maksimaal**	[maksimãl]
the largest (adj)	**die grootste**	[di χroətstə]

jerrycan	**petrolblik**
tank (e.g., tank car)	**tenk**
mug	**beker**
cup (of coffee, etc.)	**koppie**
saucer	**piering**
glass (tumbler)	**glas**
wine glass	**wynglas**
stock pot (soup pot)	**soppot**
bottle (~ of wine)	**bottel**
neck (of the bottle, etc.)	**nek**
carafe (decanter)	**kraffie**
pitcher	**kruik**
vessel (container)	**houer**
pot (crock, stoneware ~)	**pot**
vase	**vaas**
bottle (perfume ~)	**bottel**
vial, small bottle	**botteltjie**
tube (of toothpaste)	**buisie**
sack (bag)	**sak**
bag (paper ~, plastic ~)	**sak**
pack (of cigarettes, etc.)	**pakkie**
box (e.g., shoebox)	**kartondoos**
crate	**krat**
basket	**mandjie**

MAIN VERBS

13. The most important verbs. Part 1

to advise (vt)	**aanraai**	[ānrāi]
to agree (say yes)	**saamstem**	[sāmstem]
to answer (vi, vt)	**antwoord**	[antwoərt]
to apologize (vi)	**verskoning vra**	[ferskoniŋ fra]
to arrive (vi)	**aankom**	[ānkom]
to ask (~ oneself)	**vra**	[fra]
to ask (~ sb to do sth)	**vra**	[fra]
to be (vi)	**wees**	[veəs]
to be afraid	**bang wees**	[baŋ veəs]
to be hungry	**honger wees**	[honər veəs]
to be interested in ...	**belangstel in ...**	[belaŋstel in ...]
to be needed	**nodig wees**	[nodeχ veəs]
to be surprised	**verbaas wees**	[ferbās veəs]
to be thirsty	**dors wees**	[dors veəs]
to begin (vt)	**begin**	[beχin]
to belong to ...	**behoort aan ...**	[behoərt ān ...]
to boast (vi)	**spog**	[spoχ]
to break (split into pieces)	**breek**	[breək]
to call (~ for help)	**roep**	[rup]
can (v aux)	**kan**	[kan]
to catch (vt)	**vang**	[faŋ]
to change (vt)	**verander**	[ferandər]
to choose (select)	**kies**	[kis]
to come down (the stairs)	**afkom**	[afkom]
to compare (vt)	**vergelyk**	[ferχelajk]
to complain (vi, vt)	**kla**	[kla]
to confuse (mix up)	**verwar**	[ferwar]
to continue (vt)	**aangaan**	[ānχān]
to control (vt)	**kontroleer**	[kontroleər]
to cook (dinner)	**kook**	[koək]
to cost (vt)	**kos**	[kos]
to count (add up)	**tel**	[təl]
to count on ...	**reken op ...**	[reken op ...]
to create (vt)	**skep**	[skep]
to cry (weep)	**huil**	[hœil]

14. The most important verbs. Part 2

to deceive (vi, vt)	bedrieg	[bedrəχ]
to decorate (tree, street)	versier	[fersir]
to defend (a country, etc.)	verdedig	[ferdedəχ]
to demand (request firmly)	eis	[æjs]
to dig (vt)	grawe	[χravə]
to discuss (vt)	bespreek	[bespreek]
to do (vt)	doen	[dun]
to doubt (have doubts)	twyfel	[twajfəl]
to drop (let fall)	laat val	[lāt fal]
to enter (room, house, etc.)	binnegaan	[binnəχān]
to excuse (forgive)	verskoon	[ferskoən]
to exist (vi)	bestaan	[bestān]
to expect (foresee)	voorsien	[foərsin]
to explain (vt)	verduidelik	[ferdœidəlik]
to fall (vi)	val	[fal]
to find (vt)	vind	[fint]
to finish (vt)	klaarmaak	[klārmāk]
to fly (vi)	vlieg	[fliχ]
to follow ... (come after)	volg ...	[folχ ...]
to forget (vi, vt)	vergeet	[ferχeət]
to forgive (vt)	vergewe	[ferχevə]
to give (vt)	gee	[χeə]
to go (on foot)	gaan	[χān]
to go for a swim	gaan swem	[χān swem]
to go out (for dinner, etc.)	uitgaan	[œitχān]
to guess (the answer)	raai	[rāi]
to have (vt)	hê	[hɛ:]
to have breakfast	ontbyt	[ontbajt]
to have dinner	aandete gebruik	[āndetə χebrœik]
to have lunch	gaan eet	[χān eət]
to hear (vt)	hoor	[hoər]
to help (vt)	help	[hɛlp]
to hide (vt)	wegsteek	[veχsteək]
to hope (vi, vt)	hoop	[hoəp]
to hunt (vi, vt)	jag	[jaχ]
to hurry (vi)	opskud	[opskut]

15. The most important verbs. Part 3

to inform (vt)	in kennis stel	[in kɛnnis stəl]
to insist (vi, vt)	aandring	[āndriŋ]

to insult (vt)	beledig	[beledəχ]
to invite (vt)	uitnooi	[œitnoj]
to joke (vi)	grappies maak	[χrappis māk]

to keep (vt)	bewaar	[bevār]
to keep silent	stilbly	[stilblaj]
to kill (vt)	doodmaak	[doədmāk]
to know (sb)	ken	[ken]
to know (sth)	weet	[veət]
to laugh (vi)	lag	[laχ]

to liberate (city, etc.)	bevry	[befraj]
to like (I like …)	hou van	[hæʊ fan]
to look for … (search)	soek …	[suk …]
to love (sb)	liefhê	[lifhɛ:]

to manage, to run	beheer	[beheər]
to mean (signify)	beteken	[betekən]
to mention (talk about)	verwys na	[ferwajs na]
to miss (school, etc.)	bank	[bank]
to notice (see)	raaksien	[rāksin]

to object (vi, vt)	beswaar maak	[beswār māk]
to observe (see)	waarneem	[vārneəm]
to open (vt)	oopmaak	[oəpmāk]
to order (meal, etc.)	bestel	[bestəl]
to order (mil.)	beveel	[befeəl]
to own (possess)	besit	[besit]

to participate (vi)	deelneem	[deəlneəm]
to pay (vi, vt)	betaal	[betāl]
to permit (vt)	toestaan	[tustān]
to plan (vt)	beplan	[beplan]
to play (children)	speel	[speəl]

to pray (vi, vt)	bid	[bit]
to prefer (vt)	verkies	[ferkis]
to promise (vt)	beloof	[beloəf]
to pronounce (vt)	uitspreek	[œitspreək]
to propose (vt)	voorstel	[foərstəl]
to punish (vt)	straf	[straf]

16. The most important verbs. Part 4

to read (vi, vt)	lees	[leəs]
to recommend (vt)	aanbeveel	[ānbefeəl]
to refuse (vi, vt)	weier	[væjer]
to regret (be sorry)	jammer wees	[jammər veəs]
to rent (sth from sb)	huur	[hɪr]
to repeat (say again)	herhaal	[herhāl]

to reserve, to book	**bespreek**	[bespreək]
to run (vi)	**hardloop**	[hardloəp]
to save (rescue)	**red**	[ret]
to say (~ thank you)	**sê**	[sɛ:]
to scold (vt)	**uitvaar teen**	[œitfãr teən]
to see (vt)	**sien**	[sin]
to sell (vt)	**verkoop**	[ferkoəp]
to send (vt)	**stuur**	[stɪr]
to shoot (vi)	**skiet**	[skit]
to shout (vi)	**skreeu**	[skriʊ]
to show (vt)	**wys**	[vajs]
to sign (document)	**teken**	[tekən]
to sit down (vi)	**gaan sit**	[χãn sit]
to smile (vi)	**glimlag**	[χlimlaχ]
to speak (vi, vt)	**praat**	[prãt]
to steal (money, etc.)	**steel**	[steəl]
to stop (for pause, etc.)	**stilhou**	[stilhæʊ]
to stop (please ~ calling me)	**ophou**	[ophæʊ]
to study (vt)	**studeer**	[studeər]
to swim (vi)	**swem**	[swem]
to take (vt)	**vat**	[fat]
to think (vi, vt)	**dink**	[dink]
to threaten (vt)	**dreig**	[dræjχ]
to touch (with hands)	**aanraak**	[ãnrăk]
to translate (vt)	**vertaal**	[fertãl]
to trust (vt)	**vertrou**	[fertræʊ]
to try (attempt)	**probeer**	[probeər]
to turn (e.g., ~ left)	**draai**	[drãi]
to underestimate (vt)	**onderskat**	[ondərskat]
to understand (vt)	**verstaan**	[ferstãn]
to unite (vt)	**verenig**	[ferenəχ]
to wait (vt)	**wag**	[vaχ]
to want (wish, desire)	**wil**	[vil]
to warn (vt)	**waarsku**	[vãrsku]
to work (vi)	**werk**	[verk]
to write (vt)	**skryf**	[skrajf]
to write down	**opskryf**	[opskrajf]

TIME. CALENDAR

17. Weekdays

Monday	**Maandag**	[mãndaχ]
Tuesday	**Dinsdag**	[dinsdaχ]
Wednesday	**Woensdag**	[voeŋsdaχ]
Thursday	**Donderdag**	[dondərdaχ]
Friday	**Vrydag**	[frajdaχ]
Saturday	**Saterdag**	[satərdaχ]
Sunday	**Sondag**	[sondaχ]
today (adv)	**vandag**	[fandaχ]
tomorrow (adv)	**môre**	[mɔrə]
the day after tomorrow	**oormôre**	[oərmɔrə]
yesterday (adv)	**gister**	[χistər]
the day before yesterday	**eergister**	[eərχistər]
day	**dag**	[daχ]
working day	**werksdag**	[verks·daχ]
public holiday	**openbare vakansiedag**	[openbarə fakaŋsi·daχ]
day off	**verlofdag**	[ferlofdaχ]
weekend	**naweek**	[naveək]
all day long	**die hele dag**	[di helə daχ]
the next day (adv)	**die volgende dag**	[di folχendə daχ]
two days ago	**twee dae gelede**	[tweə daə χeledə]
the day before	**die dag voor**	[di daχ foər]
daily (adj)	**daeliks**	[daeliks]
every day (adv)	**elke dag**	[ɛlkə daχ]
week	**week**	[veək]
last week (adv)	**laas week**	[lãs veək]
next week (adv)	**volgende week**	[folχendə veək]
weekly (adj)	**weekliks**	[veəkliks]
every week (adv)	**weekliks**	[veəkliks]
every Tuesday	**elke Dinsdag**	[ɛlkə dinsdaχ]

18. Hours. Day and night

morning	**oggend**	[oχent]
in the morning	**soggens**	[soχɛŋs]
noon, midday	**middag**	[middaχ]
in the afternoon	**in die namiddag**	[in di namiddaχ]

evening	aand	[ãnt]
in the evening	saans	[sãŋs]
night	nag	[naχ]
at night	snags	[snaχs]
midnight	middernag	[middərnaχ]

second	sekonde	[sekondə]
minute	minuut	[minɪt]
hour	uur	[ɪr]
half an hour	n halfuur	[n halfɪr]
fifteen minutes	vyftien minute	[fajftin minutə]
24 hours	24 ure	[fir-en-twintəχ urə]

sunrise	sonop	[son·op]
dawn	daeraad	[daerãt]
early morning	elke oggend	[ɛlkə oχent]
sunset	sononder	[son·ondər]

early in the morning	vroegdag	[fruχdaχ]
this morning	vanmôre	[fanmɔrə]
tomorrow morning	môreoggend	[mɔrə·oχent]

this afternoon	vanmiddag	[fanmiddaχ]
in the afternoon	in die namiddag	[in di namiddaχ]
tomorrow afternoon	môremiddag	[mɔrə·middaχ]

tonight (this evening)	vanaand	[fanãnt]
tomorrow night	môreaand	[mɔrə·ãnt]

at 3 o'clock sharp	klokslag 3 uur	[klokslaχ dri ɪr]
about 4 o'clock	omstreeks 4 uur	[omstreeks fir ɪr]
by 12 o'clock	teen 12 uur	[teən twalf ɪr]

in 20 minutes	oor twintig minute	[oer twintəχ minutə]
on time (adv)	betyds	[betajds]

a quarter of ...	kwart voor ...	[kwart foər ...]
every 15 minutes	elke 15 minute	[ɛlkə fajftin minutə]
round the clock	24 uur per dag	[fir-en-twintəχ pər daχ]

19. Months. Seasons

January	Januarie	[januari]
February	Februarie	[februari]
March	Maart	[mãrt]
April	April	[april]
May	Mei	[mæj]
June	Junie	[juni]
July	Julie	[juli]
August	Augustus	[ɔuχustus]

September	September	[septembər]
October	Oktober	[oktobər]
November	November	[nofembər]
December	Desember	[desembər]

spring	lente	[lentə]
in spring	in die lente	[in di lentə]
spring (as adj)	lente-	[lente-]

summer	somer	[somər]
in summer	in die somer	[in di somər]
summer (as adj)	somerse	[somersə]

fall	herfs	[herfs]
in fall	in die herfs	[in di herfs]
fall (as adj)	herfsagtige	[herfsaχtiχə]

winter	winter	[vintər]
in winter	in die winter	[in di vintər]
winter (as adj)	winter-	[vintər-]

month	maand	[mānt]
this month	hierdie maand	[hirdi mānt]
next month	volgende maand	[folχendə mānt]
last month	laasmaand	[lāsmānt]
in 2 months (2 months later)	oor twe maande	[oər twe māndə]
the whole month	die hele maand	[di helə mānt]

monthly (~ magazine)	maandeliks	[māndəliks]
monthly (adv)	maandeliks	[māndəliks]
every month	elke maand	[ɛlkə mānt]

year	jaar	[jār]
this year	hierdie jaar	[hirdi jār]
next year	volgende jaar	[folχendə jār]
last year	laasjaar	[lāʃār]

| in two years | binne twee jaar | [binnə tweə jār] |
| the whole year | die hele jaar | [di helə jār] |

every year	elke jaar	[ɛlkə jār]
annual (adj)	jaarliks	[jārliks]
annually (adv)	jaarliks	[jārliks]
4 times a year	4 keer per jaar	[fir keər pər jār]

date (e.g., today's ~)	datum	[datum]
date (e.g., ~ of birth)	datum	[datum]
calendar	kalender	[kalendər]
six months	ses maande	[ses māndə]
season (summer, etc.)	seisoen	[sæjsun]
century	eeu	[iʊ]

TRAVEL. HOTEL

20. Trip. Travel

tourism, travel	**toerisme**	[turismə]
tourist	**toeris**	[turis]
trip, voyage	**reis**	[ræjs]
adventure	**avontuur**	[afontɪr]
trip, journey	**reis**	[ræjs]
vacation	**vakansie**	[fakaŋsi]
to be on vacation	**met vakansie wees**	[met fakaŋsi veəs]
rest	**rus**	[rus]
train	**trein**	[træjn]
by train	**per trein**	[pər træjn]
airplane	**vliegtuig**	[fliχtœiχ]
by airplane	**per vliegtuig**	[pər fliχtœiχ]
by car	**per motor**	[pər motor]
by ship	**per skip**	[pər skip]
luggage	**bagasie**	[baχasi]
suitcase	**tas**	[tas]
luggage cart	**bagasiekarretjie**	[baχasi·karrəki]
passport	**paspoort**	[paspoərt]
visa	**visum**	[fisum]
ticket	**kaartjie**	[kārki]
air ticket	**lugkaartjie**	[luχ·kārki]
guidebook	**reisgids**	[ræjsχids]
map (tourist ~)	**kaart**	[kārt]
area (rural ~)	**gebied**	[χebit]
place, site	**plek**	[plek]
exotica (n)	**eksotiese dinge**	[ɛksotisə diŋə]
exotic (adj)	**eksoties**	[ɛksotis]
amazing (adj)	**verbasend**	[ferbasent]
group	**groep**	[χrup]
excursion, sightseeing tour	**uitstappie**	[œitstappi]
guide (person)	**gids**	[χids]

21. Hotel

hotel	**hotel**	[hotəl]
motel	**motel**	[motəl]
three-star (~ hotel)	**drie-ster**	[dri-stər]
five-star	**vyf-ster**	[fajf-stər]
to stay (in a hotel, etc.)	**oornag**	[oərnaχ]
room	**kamer**	[kamər]
single room	**enkelkamer**	[ɛnkəl·kamər]
double room	**dubbelkamer**	[dubbəl·kamər]
half board	**met aandete,**	[met ãndetə],
	bed en ontbyt	[bet en ontbajt]
full board	**volle losies**	[follə losis]
with bath	**met bad**	[met bat]
with shower	**met stortbad**	[met stort·bat]
satellite television	**satelliet-TV**	[satɛllit-te·fe]
air-conditioner	**lugversorger**	[luχfersorχər]
towel	**handdoek**	[handduk]
key	**sleutel**	[sløətəl]
administrator	**bestuurder**	[bestɪrdər]
chambermaid	**kamermeisie**	[kamər·mæjsi]
porter, bellboy	**hoteljoggie**	[hotəl·joχi]
doorman	**portier**	[portir]
restaurant	**restaurant**	[restɔurant]
pub, bar	**kroeg**	[kruχ]
breakfast	**ontbyt**	[ontbajt]
dinner	**aandete**	[ãndetə]
buffet	**buffetete**	[buffetetə]
lobby	**voorportaal**	[foər·portãl]
elevator	**hysbak**	[hajsbak]
DO NOT DISTURB	**MOENIE STEUR NIE**	[muni støər ni]
NO SMOKING	**ROOK VERBODE**	[roək ferbodə]

22. Sightseeing

monument	**monument**	[monument]
fortress	**fort**	[fort]
palace	**paleis**	[palæjs]
castle	**kasteel**	[kasteəl]
tower	**toring**	[toriŋ]
mausoleum	**mausoleum**	[mɔusoløəm]

architecture	**argitektuur**	[arχitektɪr]
medieval (adj)	**Middeleeus**	[middeliʊs]
ancient (adj)	**oud**	[æʊt]
national (adj)	**nasionaal**	[naʃionāl]
famous (monument, etc.)	**bekend**	[bekent]

tourist	**toeris**	[turis]
guide (person)	**gids**	[χids]
excursion, sightseeing tour	**uitstappie**	[œitstappi]
to show (vt)	**wys**	[vajs]
to tell (vt)	**vertel**	[fertəl]

to find (vt)	**vind**	[fint]
to get lost (lose one's way)	**verdwaal**	[ferdwāl]
map (e.g., subway ~)	**kaart**	[kārt]
map (e.g., city ~)	**kaart**	[kārt]

souvenir, gift	**aandenking**	[āndenkiŋ]
gift shop	**geskenkwinkel**	[χeskɛnk·vinkəl]
to take pictures	**fotografeer**	[fotoχrafeər]
to have one's picture taken	**jou portret laat maak**	[jæʊ portret lāt māk]

TRANSPORTATION

23. Airport

airport	lughawe	[luχhavə]
airplane	vliegtuig	[fliχtœiχ]
airline	lugredery	[luχrederaj]
air traffic controller	lugverkeersleier	[luχ·ferkeərs·læjer]
departure	vertrek	[fertrek]
arrival	aankoms	[ānkoms]
to arrive (by plane)	aankom	[ānkom]
departure time	vertrektyd	[fertrək·tajt]
arrival time	aankomstyd	[ānkoms·tajt]
to be delayed	vertraag wees	[fertrāχ veəs]
flight delay	vlugvertraging	[fluχ·fertraχiŋ]
information board	informasiebord	[informasi·bort]
information	informasie	[informasi]
to announce (vt)	aankondig	[ānkondəχ]
flight (e.g., next ~)	vlug	[fluχ]
customs	doeane	[duanə]
customs officer	doeanebeampte	[duanə·beamptə]
customs declaration	doeaneverklaring	[duanə·ferklariŋ]
to fill out (vt)	invul	[inful]
passport control	paspoortkontrole	[paspoərt·kontrolə]
luggage	bagasie	[baχasi]
hand luggage	handbagasie	[hand·baχasi]
luggage cart	bagasiekarretjie	[baχasi·karrəki]
landing	landing	[landiŋ]
landing strip	landingsbaan	[landiŋs·bān]
to land (vi)	land	[lant]
airstairs	vliegtuigtrap	[fliχtœiχ·trap]
check-in	na die vertrektoonbank	[na di fertrək·toənbank]
check-in counter	vertrektoonbank	[fertrək·toənbank]
to check-in (vi)	na die vertrektoonbank gaan	[na di fertrək·toənbank χān]
boarding pass	instapkaart	[instap·kārt]
departure gate	vertrekuitgang	[fertrek·œitχaŋ]

transit	transito	[traŋsito]
to wait (vt)	wag	[vaχ]
departure lounge	vertreksaal	[fertrək·sāl]
to see off	afsien	[afsin]
to say goodbye	afskeid neem	[afskæjt neəm]

24. Airplane

airplane	vliegtuig	[fliχtœiχ]
air ticket	lugkaartjie	[luχ·kārki]
airline	lugredery	[luχrederaj]
airport	lughawe	[luχhavə]
supersonic (adj)	supersonies	[supersonis]

captain	kaptein	[kaptæjn]
crew	bemanning	[bemanniŋ]
pilot	piloot	[piloət]
flight attendant (fem.)	lugwaardin	[luχ·wārdin]
navigator	navigator	[nafiχator]

wings	vlerke	[flerkə]
tail	stert	[stert]
cockpit	stuurkajuit	[stɪr·kajœit]
engine	enjin	[ɛnʤin]
undercarriage (landing gear)	landingstel	[landiŋ·stəl]
turbine	turbine	[turbinə]

propeller	skroef	[skruf]
black box	swart boks	[swart boks]
yoke (control column)	stuurstang	[stɪr·staŋ]
fuel	brandstof	[brantstof]

safety card	veiligheidskaart	[fæjliχæjts·kārt]
oxygen mask	suurstofmasker	[sɪrstof·maskər]
uniform	uniform	[uniform]
life vest	reddingsbaadjie	[rɛddiŋs·bāʤi]
parachute	valskerm	[fal·skerm]

takeoff	opstyging	[opstajχiŋ]
to take off (vi)	opstyg	[opstajχ]
runway	landingsbaan	[landiŋs·bān]

visibility	uitsig	[œitsəχ]
flight (act of flying)	vlug	[fluχ]
altitude	hoogte	[hoeχtə]
air pocket	lugsak	[luχsak]

| seat | sitplek | [sitplek] |
| headphones | koptelefoon | [kop·telefoən] |

folding tray (tray table)	voutafeltjie	[fæʊ·tafɛlki]
airplane window	vliegtuigvenster	[fliχtœiχ·fɛŋstər]
aisle	paadjie	[pãdʒi]

25. Train

train	trein	[træjn]
commuter train	voorstedelike trein	[foərstedelikə træjn]
express train	sneltrein	[snɛl·træjn]
diesel locomotive	diesellokomotief	[disəl·lokomotif]
steam locomotive	stoomlokomotief	[stoəm·lokomotif]

| passenger car | passasierswa | [passasirs·wa] |
| dining car | eetwa | [eət·wa] |

rails	spoorstawe	[spoər·stavə]
railroad	spoorweg	[spoər·weχ]
railway tie	dwarslêer	[dwarslɛər]

platform (railway ~)	perron	[perron]
track (~ 1, 2, etc.)	spoor	[spoər]
semaphore	semafoor	[semafoər]
station	stasie	[stasi]

engineer (train driver)	treindrywer	[træjn·drajvər]
porter (of luggage)	portier	[portir]
car attendant	kondukteur	[konduktøər]
passenger	passasier	[passasir]
conductor (ticket inspector)	kondukteur	[konduktøər]

| corridor (in train) | gang | [χaŋ] |
| emergency brake | noodrem | [noədrem] |

compartment	kompartiment	[kompartiment]
berth	bed	[bet]
upper berth	boonste bed	[boəŋstə bet]
lower berth	onderste bed	[ondərstə bet]
bed linen, bedding	beddegoed	[beddə·χut]

ticket	kaartjie	[kãrki]
schedule	diensrooster	[diŋs·roəstər]
information display	informasiebord	[informasi·bort]

to leave, to depart	vertrek	[fertrek]
departure (of train)	vertrek	[fertrek]
to arrive (ab. train)	aankom	[ãnkom]
arrival	aankoms	[ãnkoms]
to arrive by train	aankom per trein	[ãnkom pər træjn]
to get on the train	in die trein klim	[in di træjn klim]

to get off the train	uit die trein klim	[œit di træjn klim]
train wreck	treinbotsing	[træjn·botsiŋ]
to derail (vi)	ontspoor	[ontspoər]

steam locomotive	stoomlokomotief	[stoəm·lokomotif]
stoker, fireman	stoker	[stokər]
firebox	stookplek	[stoəkplɛk]
coal	steenkool	[steən·koəl]

26. Ship

| ship | skip | [skip] |
| vessel | vaartuig | [fārtœiχ] |

steamship	stoomboot	[stoəm·boət]
riverboat	rivierboot	[rifir·boət]
cruise ship	toerskip	[tur·skip]
cruiser	kruiser	[krœisər]

yacht	jag	[jaχ]
tugboat	sleepboot	[sleəp·boət]
barge	vragskuit	[fraχ·skœit]
ferry	veerboot	[feər·boət]

| sailing ship | seilskip | [sæjl·skip] |
| brigantine | skoenerbrik | [skunər·brik] |

| ice breaker | ysbreker | [ajs·brekər] |
| submarine | duikboot | [dœik·boət] |

boat (flat-bottomed ~)	roeiboot	[ruiboət]
dinghy	bootjie	[boəki]
lifeboat	reddingsboot	[rɛddiŋs·boət]
motorboat	motorboot	[motor·boət]

captain	kaptein	[kaptæjn]
seaman	seeman	[seəman]
sailor	matroos	[matroəs]
crew	bemanning	[bemanniŋ]

boatswain	bootsman	[boətsman]
ship's boy	skeepsjonge	[skeəps·joŋə]
cook	kok	[kok]
ship's doctor	skeepsdokter	[skeəps·doktər]

deck	dek	[dek]
mast	mas	[mas]
sail	seil	[sæjl]
hold	skeepsruim	[skeəps·rœim]
bow (prow)	boeg	[buχ]

stern	agterstewe	[aχtərstevə]
oar	roeispaan	[ruis·pãn]
screw propeller	skroef	[skruf]

cabin	kajuit	[kajœit]
wardroom	offisierskajuit	[offisirs·kajœit]
engine room	enjinkamer	[ɛndʒin·kamər]
bridge	brug	[bruχ]
radio room	radiokamer	[radio·kamər]
wave (radio)	golf	[χolf]
logbook	logboek	[loχbuk]

spyglass	verkyker	[ferkajkər]
bell	bel	[bəl]
flag	vlag	[flaχ]

| hawser (mooring ~) | kabel | [kabəl] |
| knot (bowline, etc.) | knoop | [knoəp] |

| deckrails | dekleuning | [dek·løəniŋ] |
| gangway | gangplank | [χaŋ·plank] |

anchor	anker	[ankər]
to weigh anchor	anker lig	[ankər ləχ]
to drop anchor	anker uitgooi	[ankər œitχoj]
anchor chain	ankerketting	[ankər·kɛttiŋ]

port (harbor)	hawe	[havə]
quay, wharf	kaai	[kãi]
to berth (moor)	vasmeer	[fasmeər]
to cast off	vertrek	[fertrek]

trip, voyage	reis	[ræjs]
cruise (sea trip)	cruise	[kruːs]
course (route)	koers	[kurs]
route (itinerary)	roete	[rutə]

fairway (safe water channel)	vaarwater	[fãr·vatər]
shallows	sandbank	[sand·bank]
to run aground	strand	[strant]

storm	storm	[storm]
signal	sienjaal	[sinjãl]
to sink (vi)	sink	[sink]
Man overboard!	Man oorboord!	[man oərboərd!]
SOS (distress signal)	SOS	[sos]
ring buoy	reddingsboei	[rɛddiŋs·bui]

CITY

27. Urban transportation

bus	**bus**	[bus]
streetcar	**trem**	[trem]
trolley bus	**trembus**	[trembus]
route (of bus, etc.)	**busroete**	[bus·rutə]
number (e.g., bus ~)	**nommer**	[nommər]
to go by ...	**ry per ...**	[raj pər ...]
to get on (~ the bus)	**inklim**	[inklim]
to get off ...	**uitklim ...**	[œitklim ...]
stop (e.g., bus ~)	**halte**	[haltə]
next stop	**volgende halte**	[folχendə haltə]
terminus	**eindpunt**	[æjnd·punt]
schedule	**diensrooster**	[diŋs·roəstər]
to wait (vt)	**wag**	[vaχ]
ticket	**kaartjie**	[kārki]
fare	**reistarief**	[ræjs·tarif]
cashier (ticket seller)	**kaartjieverkoper**	[kārki·ferkopər]
ticket inspection	**kaartjiekontrole**	[kārki·kontrolə]
ticket inspector	**kontroleur**	[kontroløər]
to be late (for ...)	**laat wees**	[lāt veəs]
to miss (~ the train, etc.)	**mis**	[mis]
to be in a hurry	**haastig wees**	[hāstəχ veəs]
taxi, cab	**taxi**	[taksi]
taxi driver	**taxibestuurder**	[taksi·bestɪrdər]
by taxi	**per taxi**	[pər taksi]
taxi stand	**taxistaanplek**	[taksi·stānplek]
traffic	**verkeer**	[ferkeər]
traffic jam	**verkeersknoop**	[ferkeərs·knoəp]
rush hour	**spitsuur**	[spits·ɪr]
to park (vi)	**parkeer**	[parkeər]
to park (vt)	**parkeer**	[parkeər]
parking lot	**parkeerterrein**	[parkeər·terræjn]
subway	**metro**	[metro]
station	**stasie**	[stasi]
to take the subway	**die metro vat**	[di metro fat]

| train | trein | [træjn] |
| train station | treinstasie | [træjn·stasi] |

28. City. Life in the city

city, town	stad	[stat]
capital city	hoofstad	[hoəf·stat]
village	dorp	[dorp]

city map	stadskaart	[stats·kãrt]
downtown	sentrum	[sentrum]
suburb	voorstad	[foərstat]
suburban (adj)	voorstedelik	[foərstedelik]

outskirts	buitewyke	[bœitəvajkə]
environs (suburbs)	omgewing	[omχeviŋ]
city block	stadswyk	[stats·wajk]
residential block (area)	woonbuurt	[voənbɪrt]

traffic	verkeer	[ferkeər]
traffic lights	robot	[robot]
public transportation	openbare vervoer	[openbarə ferfur]
intersection	kruispunt	[krœis·punt]

crosswalk	sebraoorgang	[sebra·oərχaŋ]
pedestrian underpass	voetgangertonnel	[futχaŋər·tonnəl]
to cross (~ the street)	oorsteek	[oərsteək]
pedestrian	voetganger	[futχaŋər]
sidewalk	sypaadjie	[saj·pãdʒi]

bridge	brug	[bruχ]
embankment (river walk)	wal	[val]
fountain	fontein	[fontæjn]

allée (garden walkway)	laning	[laniŋ]
park	park	[park]
boulevard	boulevard	[bulefar]
square	plein	[plæjn]
avenue (wide street)	laan	[lãn]
street	straat	[strãt]
side street	systraat	[saj·strãt]
dead end	doodloopstraat	[doədloəp·strãt]

house	huis	[hœis]
building	gebou	[χebæʊ]
skyscraper	wolkekrabber	[volkə·krabbər]

facade	gewel	[χevəl]
roof	dak	[dak]
window	venster	[fɛŋstər]

arch	arkade	[arkadə]
column	kolom	[kolom]
corner	hoek	[huk]

store window	uitstalraam	[œitstalrām]
signboard (store sign, etc.)	reklamebord	[reklamə·bort]
poster	plakkaat	[plakkāt]
advertising poster	reklameplakkaat	[reklamə·plakkāt]
billboard	aanplakbord	[ānplakbort]

garbage, trash	vullis	[fullis]
trashcan (public ~)	vullisbak	[fullis·bak]
to litter (vi)	rommel strooi	[rommel stroj]
garbage dump	vullishoop	[fullis·hoəp]

phone booth	telefoonhokkie	[telefoən·hokki]
lamppost	lamppaal	[lamp·pāl]
bench (park ~)	bank	[bank]

police officer	polisieman	[polisi·man]
police	polisie	[polisi]
beggar	bedelaar	[bedelār]
homeless (n)	daklose	[daklosə]

29. Urban institutions

store	winkel	[vinkəl]
drugstore, pharmacy	apteek	[apteək]
eyeglass store	optisiên	[optisiɛn]
shopping mall	winkelsentrum	[vinkəl·sentrum]
supermarket	supermark	[supermark]

bakery	bakkery	[bakkeraj]
baker	bakker	[bakkər]
pastry shop	banketbakkery	[banket·bakkeraj]
grocery store	kruidenierswinkel	[krœidenirs·vinkəl]
butcher shop	slagter	[slaχtər]

| produce store | groentewinkel | [χruntə·vinkəl] |
| market | mark | [mark] |

coffee house	koffiekroeg	[koffi·kruχ]
restaurant	restaurant	[restɔurant]
pub, bar	kroeg	[kruχ]
pizzeria	pizzeria	[pizzeria]

hair salon	haarsalon	[hār·salon]
post office	poskantoor	[pos·kantoər]
dry cleaners	droogskoonmakers	[droəχ·skoən·makers]
photo studio	fotostudio	[foto·studio]

shoe store	skoenwinkel	[skun·vinkəl]
bookstore	boekhandel	[buk·handəl]
sporting goods store	sportwinkel	[sport·vinkəl]

clothes repair shop	klereherstelwinkel	[klerə·herstəl·vinkəl]
formal wear rental	klereverhuurwinkel	[klerə·ferhɪr·vinkəl]
video rental store	videowinkel	[video·vinkəl]

circus	sirkus	[sirkus]
zoo	dieretuin	[dirə·tœin]
movie theater	bioskoop	[bioskoəp]
museum	museum	[musøəm]
library	biblioteek	[biblioteək]

theater	teater	[teatər]
opera (opera house)	opera	[opera]
nightclub	nagklub	[naχ·klup]
casino	kasino	[kasino]

mosque	moskee	[moskeə]
synagogue	sinagoge	[sinaχoχə]
cathedral	katedraal	[katedrãl]
temple	tempel	[tempəl]
church	kerk	[kerk]

college	kollege	[kolledʒ]
university	universiteit	[unifersitæjt]
school	skool	[skoəl]

prefecture	stadhuis	[stat·hœis]
city hall	stadhuis	[stat·hœis]
hotel	hotel	[hotəl]
bank	bank	[bank]

embassy	ambassade	[ambassadə]
travel agency	reisagentskap	[ræjs·aχentskap]
information office	inligtingskantoor	[inliχtiŋs·kantoər]
currency exchange	wisselkantoor	[vissəl·kantoər]

| subway | metro | [metro] |
| hospital | hospitaal | [hospitãl] |

| gas station | petrolstasie | [petrol·stasi] |
| parking lot | parkeerterrein | [parkeər·terræjn] |

30. Signs

signboard (store sign, etc.)	reklamebord	[reklamə·bort]
notice (door sign, etc.)	kennisgewing	[kɛnnis·χeviŋ]
poster	plakkaat	[plakkãt]

| direction sign | **rigtingwyser** | [riχtiŋ·wajsər] |
| arrow (sign) | **pyl** | [pajl] |

caution	**waarskuwing**	[vārskuviŋ]
warning sign	**waarskuwingsbord**	[vārskuviŋs·bort]
to warn (vt)	**waarsku**	[vārsku]

rest day (weekly ~)	**rusdag**	[rusdaχ]
timetable (schedule)	**diensrooster**	[diŋs·roəstər]
opening hours	**besigheidsure**	[besiχæjts·urə]

WELCOME!	**WELKOM!**	[vɛlkom!]
ENTRANCE	**INGANG**	[inχaŋ]
EXIT	**UITGANG**	[œitχaŋ]

| PUSH | **STOOT** | [stoət] |
| PULL | **TREK** | [trek] |

| OPEN | **OOP** | [oəp] |
| CLOSED | **GESLUIT** | [χeslœit] |

| WOMEN | **DAMES** | [dames] |
| MEN | **MANS** | [maŋs] |

| DISCOUNTS | **AFSLAG** | [afslaχ] |
| SALE | **UITVERKOPING** | [œitferkopiŋ] |

| NEW! | **NUUT!** | [nɪt!] |
| FREE | **GRATIS** | [χratis] |

ATTENTION!	**PAS OP!**	[pas op!]
NO VACANCIES	**VOLBESPREEK**	[folbespreək]
RESERVED	**BESPREEK**	[bespreək]

| ADMINISTRATION | **ADMINISTRASIE** | [administrasi] |
| STAFF ONLY | **SLEGS PERSONEEL** | [sleχs personeəl] |

BEWARE OF THE DOG!	**PAS OP VIR DIE HOND!**	[pas op fir di hont!]
NO SMOKING	**ROOK VERBODE**	[roək ferbodə]
DO NOT TOUCH!	**NIE AANRAAK NIE!**	[ni ānrāk ni!]

DANGEROUS	**GEVAARLIK**	[χefārlik]
DANGER	**GEVAAR**	[χefār]
HIGH VOLTAGE	**HOOGSPANNING**	[hoəχ·spanniŋ]

| NO SWIMMING! | **NIE SWEM NIE** | [ni swem ni] |
| OUT OF ORDER | **BUITE WERKING** | [bœitə verkiŋ] |

FLAMMABLE	**ONTVLAMBAAR**	[ontflambār]
FORBIDDEN	**VERBODE**	[ferbodə]
NO TRESPASSING!	**TOEGANG VERBODE!**	[tuχaŋ ferbode!]
WET PAINT	**NAT VERF**	[nat ferf]

31. Shopping

to buy (purchase)	**koop**	[koəp]
purchase	**aankoop**	[ānkoəp]
to go shopping	**inkopies doen**	[inkopis dun]
shopping	**inkoop**	[inkoəp]
to be open (ab. store)	**oop wees**	[oəp veəs]
to be closed	**toe wees**	[tu veəs]
footwear, shoes	**skoeisel**	[skuisəl]
clothes, clothing	**klere**	[klerə]
cosmetics	**kosmetika**	[kosmetika]
food products	**voedingsware**	[fudiŋs·warə]
gift, present	**present**	[present]
salesman	**verkoper**	[ferkopər]
saleswoman	**verkoopsdame**	[ferkoəps·damə]
check out, cash desk	**kassier**	[kassir]
mirror	**spieël**	[spiɛl]
counter (store ~)	**toonbank**	[toən·bank]
fitting room	**paskamer**	[pas·kamər]
to try on	**aanpas**	[ānpas]
to fit (ab. dress, etc.)	**pas**	[pas]
to like (I like …)	**hou van**	[hæʊ fan]
price	**prys**	[prajs]
price tag	**pryskaartjie**	[prajs·kārki]
to cost (vt)	**kos**	[kos]
How much?	**Hoeveel?**	[hufeəl?]
discount	**afslag**	[afslaχ]
inexpensive (adj)	**billik**	[billik]
cheap (adj)	**goedkoop**	[χudkoəp]
expensive (adj)	**duur**	[dɪr]
It's expensive	**dis duur**	[dis dɪr]
rental (n)	**verhuur**	[ferhɪr]
to rent (~ a tuxedo)	**verhuur**	[ferhɪr]
credit (trade credit)	**krediet**	[krediet]
on credit (adv)	**op krediet**	[op krediet]

CLOTHING & ACCESSORIES

32. Outerwear. Coats

clothes	**klere**	[klerə]
outerwear	**oorklere**	[oərklerə]
winter clothing	**winterklere**	[vintər·klerə]
coat (overcoat)	**jas**	[jas]
fur coat	**pelsjas**	[pelʃas]
fur jacket	**kort pelsjas**	[kort pelʃas]
down coat	**donsjas**	[donʃas]
jacket (e.g., leather ~)	**baadjie**	[bādʒi]
raincoat (trenchcoat, etc.)	**reënjas**	[reɛnjas]
waterproof (adj)	**waterdig**	[vatərdəχ]

33. Men's & women's clothing

shirt (button shirt)	**hemp**	[hemp]
pants	**broek**	[bruk]
jeans	**denimbroek**	[denim·bruk]
suit jacket	**baadjie**	[bādʒi]
suit	**pak**	[pak]
dress (frock)	**rok**	[rok]
skirt	**romp**	[romp]
blouse	**bloes**	[blus]
knitted jacket (cardigan, etc.)	**gebreide baadjie**	[χebræjdə bādʒi]
jacket (of woman's suit)	**baadjie**	[bādʒi]
T-shirt	**T-hemp**	[te-hemp]
shorts (short trousers)	**kortbroek**	[kort·bruk]
tracksuit	**sweetpak**	[sweet·pak]
bathrobe	**badjas**	[batjas]
pajamas	**pajama**	[pajama]
sweater	**trui**	[trœi]
pullover	**trui**	[trœi]
vest	**onderbaadjie**	[ondər·bādʒi]
tailcoat	**swaelstertbaadjie**	[swaɛlstert·bādʒi]
tuxedo	**aandpak**	[āntpak]

uniform	**uniform**	[uniform]
workwear	**werksklere**	[verks·klerə]
overalls	**oorpak**	[oərpak]
coat (e.g., doctor's smock)	**jas**	[jas]

34. Clothing. Underwear

underwear	**onderklere**	[ondərklerə]
boxers, briefs	**onderbroek**	[ondərbruk]
panties	**onderbroek**	[ondərbruk]
undershirt (A-shirt)	**frokkie**	[frokki]
socks	**sokkies**	[sokkis]
nightgown	**nagrok**	[naχrok]
bra	**bra**	[bra]
knee highs (knee-high socks)	**kniekouse**	[kni·kæʊsə]
pantyhose	**kousbroek**	[kæʊsbruk]
stockings (thigh highs)	**kouse**	[kæʊsə]
bathing suit	**baaikostuum**	[bãj·kostɪm]

35. Headwear

hat	**hoed**	[hut]
fedora	**hoed**	[hut]
baseball cap	**bofbalpet**	[bofbal·pet]
flatcap	**pet**	[pet]
beret	**mus**	[mus]
hood	**kap**	[kap]
panama hat	**panamahoed**	[panama·hut]
knit cap (knitted hat)	**gebreide mus**	[χebræjdə mus]
headscarf	**kopdoek**	[kopduk]
women's hat	**dameshoed**	[dames·hut]
hard hat	**veiligheidshelm**	[fæjliχæjts·hɛlm]
garrison cap	**mus**	[mus]
helmet	**helmet**	[hɛlmet]
derby	**bolhoed**	[bolhut]
top hat	**hoëhoed**	[hoɛhut]

36. Footwear

footwear	**skoeisel**	[skuisəl]
shoes (men's shoes)	**mansskoene**	[maŋs·skunə]

shoes (women's shoes)	**damesskoene**	[dames·skunə]
boots (e.g., cowboy ~)	**laarse**	[lãrsə]
slippers	**pantoffels**	[pantoffəls]
tennis shoes (e.g., Nike ~)	**tennisskoene**	[tɛnnis·skunə]
sneakers	**tekkies**	[tɛkkis]
(e.g., Converse ~)		
sandals	**sandale**	[sandalə]
cobbler (shoe repairer)	**skoenmaker**	[skun·makər]
heel	**hak**	[hak]
pair (of shoes)	**paar**	[pãr]
shoestring	**skoenveter**	[skun·fetər]
to lace (vt)	**ryg**	[rajχ]
shoehorn	**skoenlepel**	[skun·lepəl]
shoe polish	**skoenpolitoer**	[skun·politur]

37. Personal accessories

gloves	**handskoene**	[handskunə]
mittens	**duimhandskoene**	[dœim·handskunə]
scarf (muffler)	**serp**	[serp]
glasses (eyeglasses)	**bril**	[bril]
frame (eyeglass ~)	**raam**	[rãm]
umbrella	**sambreel**	[sambreəl]
walking stick	**wandelstok**	[vandəl·stok]
hairbrush	**haarborsel**	[hãr·borsəl]
fan	**waaier**	[vãjer]
tie (necktie)	**das**	[das]
bow tie	**strikkie**	[strikki]
suspenders	**kruisbande**	[krœis·bandə]
handkerchief	**sakdoek**	[sakduk]
comb	**kam**	[kam]
barrette	**haarspeld**	[hãrs·pɛlt]
hairpin	**haarpen**	[hãr·pen]
buckle	**gespe**	[χespə]
belt	**belt**	[bɛlt]
shoulder strap	**skouerband**	[skæuer·bant]
bag (handbag)	**handsak**	[hand·sak]
purse	**beursie**	[bøərsi]
backpack	**rugsak**	[ruχsak]

38. Clothing. Miscellaneous

fashion	**mode**	[modə]
in vogue (adj)	**in die mode**	[in di modə]
fashion designer	**modeontwerper**	[modə·ontwerpər]
collar	**kraag**	[krãχ]
pocket	**sak**	[sak]
pocket (as adj)	**sak-**	[sak-]
sleeve	**mou**	[mæʊ]
hanging loop	**lussie**	[lussi]
fly (on trousers)	**gulp**	[χulp]
zipper (fastener)	**ritssluiter**	[rits·slœitər]
fastener	**vasmaker**	[fasmakər]
button	**knoop**	[knoəp]
buttonhole	**knoopsgat**	[knoəps·χat]
to come off (ab. button)	**loskom**	[loskom]
to sew (vi, vt)	**naai**	[nãi]
to embroider (vi, vt)	**borduur**	[bordɪr]
embroidery	**borduurwerk**	[bordɪr·werk]
sewing needle	**naald**	[nãlt]
thread	**garing**	[χariŋ]
seam	**soom**	[soəm]
to get dirty (vi)	**vuil word**	[fœil vort]
stain (mark, spot)	**vlek**	[flek]
to crease, crumple (vi)	**kreukel**	[krøəkəl]
to tear, to rip (vt)	**skeur**	[skøər]
clothes moth	**mot**	[mot]

39. Personal care. Cosmetics

toothpaste	**tandepasta**	[tandə·pasta]
toothbrush	**tandeborsel**	[tandə·borsəl]
to brush one's teeth	**tande borsel**	[tandə borsəl]
razor	**skeermes**	[skeər·mes]
shaving cream	**skeerroom**	[skeər·roəm]
to shave (vi)	**skeer**	[skeər]
soap	**seep**	[seəp]
shampoo	**sjampoe**	[ʃampu]
scissors	**skèr**	[skær]
nail file	**naelvyl**	[naɛl·fajl]
nail clippers	**naelknipper**	[naɛl·knippər]
tweezers	**haartangetjie**	[hãrtaŋeki]

cosmetics	kosmetika	[kosmetika]
face mask	gesigmasker	[ɣesiχ·maskər]
manicure	manikuur	[manikɪr]
to have a manicure	laat manikuur	[lāt manikɪr]
pedicure	voetbehandeling	[fut·behandeliŋ]
make-up bag	kosmetika tassie	[kosmetika tassi]
face powder	gesigpoeier	[ɣesiχ·pujer]
powder compact	poeierdosie	[pujer·dosi]
blusher	blosser	[blossər]
perfume (bottled)	parfuum	[parfɪm]
toilet water (lotion)	reukwater	[røək·vatər]
lotion	vloeiroom	[flui·roəm]
cologne	reukwater	[røək·vatər]
eyeshadow	oogskadu	[oəχ·skadu]
eyeliner	oogomlyner	[oəχ·omlajnər]
mascara	maskara	[maskara]
lipstick	lipstiffie	[lip·stiffi]
nail polish, enamel	naellak	[naɛl·lak]
hair spray	haarsproei	[hārs·prui]
deodorant	reukweermiddel	[røək·veərmiddəl]
cream	room	[roəm]
face cream	gesigroom	[ɣesiχ·roəm]
hand cream	handroom	[hand·roəm]
anti-wrinkle cream	antirimpelroom	[antirimpəl·roəm]
day cream	dagroom	[daχ·roəm]
night cream	nagroom	[naχ·roəm]
day (as adj)	dag-	[daχ-]
night (as adj)	nag-	[naχ-]
tampon	tampon	[tampon]
toilet paper (toilet roll)	toiletpapier	[tojlet·papir]
hair dryer	haardroër	[hār·droɛr]

40. Watches. Clocks

watch (wristwatch)	polshorlosie	[pols·horlosi]
dial	wyserplaat	[vajsər·plāt]
hand (of clock, watch)	wyster	[vajstər]
metal watch band	metaal horlosiebandjie	[metāl horlosi·bandʒi]
watch strap	horlosiebandjie	[horlosi·bandʒi]
battery	battery	[battəraj]
to be dead (battery)	pap wees	[pap veəs]
to run fast	voorloop	[foərloəp]
to run slow	agterloop	[aχtərloəp]

wall clock	**muurhorlosie**	[mɪr·horlosi]
hourglass	**uurglas**	[ɪr·χlas]
sundial	**sonwyser**	[son·wajsər]
alarm clock	**wekker**	[vɛkkər]
watchmaker	**horlosiemaker**	[horlosi·makər]
to repair (vt)	**herstel**	[herstəl]

EVERYDAY EXPERIENCE

41. Money

money	**geld**	[xɛlt]
currency exchange	**valutaruil**	[faluta·rœil]
exchange rate	**wisselkoers**	[vissəl·kurs]
ATM	**OTM**	[o·te·em]
coin	**muntstuk**	[muntstuk]
dollar	**dollar**	[dollar]
euro	**euro**	[øəro]
lira	**lira**	[lira]
Deutschmark	**Duitse mark**	[dœitsə mark]
franc	**frank**	[frank]
pound sterling	**pond sterling**	[pont sterliŋ]
yen	**yen**	[jɛn]
debt	**skuld**	[skult]
debtor	**skuldenaar**	[skuldenãr]
to lend (money)	**uitleen**	[œitleən]
to borrow (vi, vt)	**leen**	[leən]
bank	**bank**	[bank]
account	**rekening**	[rekəniŋ]
to deposit (vt)	**deponeer**	[deponeər]
to withdraw (vt)	**trek**	[trek]
credit card	**kredietkaart**	[kredit·kãrt]
cash	**kontant**	[kontant]
check	**tjek**	[tʃek]
checkbook	**tjekboek**	[tʃek·buk]
wallet	**beursie**	[bøərsi]
change purse	**muntstukbeursie**	[muntstuk·bøərsi]
safe	**brandkas**	[brant·kas]
heir	**erfgenaam**	[ɛrfχənãm]
inheritance	**erfenis**	[ɛrfenis]
fortune (wealth)	**fortuin**	[fortœin]
lease	**huur**	[hɪr]
rent (money)	**huur**	[hɪr]
to rent (sth from sb)	**huur**	[hɪr]
price	**prys**	[prajs]

| cost | **prys** | [prajs] |
| sum | **som** | [som] |

to spend (vt)	**spandeer**	[spandeər]
expenses	**onkoste**	[onkostə]
to economize (vi, vt)	**besuinig**	[besœinəχ]
economical	**ekonomies**	[ɛkonomis]

to pay (vi, vt)	**betaal**	[betãl]
payment	**betaling**	[betaliŋ]
change (give the ~)	**wisselgeld**	[vissəl·χɛlt]

tax	**belasting**	[belastiŋ]
fine	**boete**	[butə]
to fine (vt)	**beboet**	[bebut]

42. Post. Postal service

post office	**poskantoor**	[pos·kantoər]
mail (letters, etc.)	**pos**	[pos]
mailman	**posbode**	[pos·bodə]
opening hours	**besigheidsure**	[besiχæjts·urə]

letter	**brief**	[brif]
registered letter	**geregistreerde brief**	[χereχistreərdə brif]
postcard	**poskaart**	[pos·kãrt]
telegram	**telegram**	[teleχram]
package (parcel)	**pakkie**	[pakki]
money transfer	**geldoorplasing**	[χɛld·oərplasiŋ]

to receive (vt)	**ontvang**	[ontfaŋ]
to send (vt)	**stuur**	[stɪr]
sending	**versending**	[fersendiŋ]

address	**adres**	[adres]
ZIP code	**poskode**	[pos·kodə]
sender	**sender**	[sendər]
receiver	**ontvanger**	[ontfaŋer]

| name (first name) | **voornaam** | [foərnãm] |
| surname (last name) | **van** | [fan] |

postage rate	**postarief**	[pos·tarif]
standard (adj)	**standaard**	[standãrt]
economical (adj)	**ekonomies**	[ɛkonomis]

weight	**gewig**	[χevəχ]
to weigh (~ letters)	**weeg**	[veeχ]
envelope	**koevert**	[kufert]
postage stamp	**posseël**	[pos·seɛl]

43. Banking

bank	**bank**	[baŋk]
branch (of bank, etc.)	**tak**	[tak]
bank clerk, consultant	**bankklerk**	[baŋk·klɛrk]
manager (director)	**bestuurder**	[bestɪrdər]
bank account	**bankrekening**	[baŋk·rekəniŋ]
account number	**rekeningnommer**	[rekəniŋ·nommər]
checking account	**tjekrekening**	[ʧek·rekəniŋ]
savings account	**spaarrekening**	[spãr·rekəniŋ]
to close the account	**die rekening sluit**	[di rekəniŋ slœit]
to withdraw (vt)	**trek**	[trek]
deposit	**deposito**	[deposito]
wire transfer	**telegrafiese oorplasing**	[teleχrafisə oərplasiŋ]
to wire, to transfer	**oorplaas**	[oərplãs]
sum	**som**	[som]
How much?	**Hoeveel?**	[hufeəl?]
signature	**handtekening**	[hand·tekəniŋ]
to sign (vt)	**onderteken**	[ondərtekən]
credit card	**kredietkaart**	[kredit·kãrt]
code (PIN code)	**kode**	[kodə]
credit card number	**kredietkaartnommer**	[kredit·kãrt·nommər]
ATM	**OTM**	[o·te·em]
check	**tjek**	[ʧek]
checkbook	**tjekboek**	[ʧek·buk]
loan (bank ~)	**lening**	[leniŋ]
guarantee	**waarborg**	[vãrborχ]

44. Telephone. Phone conversation

telephone	**telefoon**	[telefoən]
cell phone	**selfoon**	[sɛlfoən]
answering machine	**antwoordmasjien**	[antwoərt·maʃin]
to call (by phone)	**bel**	[bəl]
phone call	**oproep**	[oprup]
Hello!	**Hallo!**	[hallo!]
to ask (vt)	**vra**	[fra]
to answer (vi, vt)	**antwoord**	[antwoərt]

to hear (vt)	hoor	[hoər]
well (adv)	goed	[χut]
not well (adv)	nie goed nie	[ni χut ni]
noises (interference)	steurings	[støəriŋs]

receiver	gehoorstuk	[χehoərstuk]
to pick up (~ the phone)	optel	[optəl]
to hang up (~ the phone)	afskakel	[afskakəl]

busy (engaged)	besig	[besəχ]
to ring (ab. phone)	lui	[lœi]
telephone book	telefoongids	[telefoən·χids]

local (adj)	lokale	[lokalə]
local call	lokale oproep	[lokalə oprup]
long distance (~ call)	langafstand	[lanχ·afstant]
long-distance call	langafstand oproep	[lanχ·afstant oprup]
international (adj)	internasionale	[internaʃionalə]
international call	internasionale oproep	[internaʃionalə oprup]

45. Cell phone

cell phone	selfoon	[sɛlfoən]
display	skerm	[skerm]
button	knoppie	[knoppi]
SIM card	SIMkaart	[sim·kãrt]

battery	battery	[battəraj]
to be dead (battery)	pap wees	[pap vees]
charger	batterylaaier	[battəraj·lajer]

menu	spyskaart	[spajs·kãrt]
settings	instellings	[instɛlliŋs]
tune (melody)	wysie	[vajsi]
to select (vt)	kies	[kis]

calculator	sakrekenaar	[sakrekənãr]
voice mail	stempos	[stem·pos]
alarm clock	wekker	[vɛkkər]
contacts	kontakte	[kontaktə]

| SMS (text message) | SMS | [es·em·es] |
| subscriber | intekenaar | [intekənãr] |

46. Stationery

| ballpoint pen | bolpen | [bol·pen] |
| fountain pen | vulpen | [ful·pen] |

pencil	potlood	[potloət]
highlighter	merkpen	[merk·pen]
felt-tip pen	viltpen	[filt·pen]

| notepad | notaboekie | [nota·buki] |
| agenda (diary) | dagboek | [daχ·buk] |

ruler	liniaal	[liniāl]
calculator	sakrekenaar	[sakrekənār]
eraser	uitveêr	[œitfɛɛr]
thumbtack	duimspyker	[dœim·spajkər]
paper clip	skuifspeld	[skœif·spɛlt]

glue	gom	[χom]
stapler	krammasjien	[kram·maʃin]
hole punch	ponsmasjien	[pɔŋs·maʃin]
pencil sharpener	skerpmaker	[skerp·makər]

47. Foreign languages

language	taal	[tāl]
foreign (adj)	vreemd	[freəmt]
foreign language	vreemde taal	[freəmdə tāl]
to study (vt)	studeer	[studeər]
to learn (language, etc.)	leer	[leər]

to read (vi, vt)	lees	[leəs]
to speak (vi, vt)	praat	[prāt]
to understand (vt)	verstaan	[ferstān]
to write (vt)	skryf	[skrajf]

fast (adv)	vinnig	[finnəχ]
slowly (adv)	stadig	[stadəχ]
fluently (adv)	vlot	[flot]

rules	reêls	[reɛls]
grammar	grammatika	[χrammatika]
vocabulary	woordeskat	[voərdeskat]
phonetics	fonetika	[fonetika]

textbook	handboek	[hand·buk]
dictionary	woordeboek	[voərdə·buk]
teach-yourself book	selfstudie boek	[sɛlfstudi buk]
phrasebook	taalgids	[tāl·χids]

cassette, tape	kasset	[kasset]
videotape	videoband	[video·bant]
CD, compact disc	CD	[se·de]
DVD	DVD	[de·fe·de]
alphabet	alfabet	[alfabet]

to spell (vt)	spel	[spel]
pronunciation	uitspraak	[œitsprāk]
accent	aksent	[aksent]

| word | woord | [voərt] |
| meaning | betekenis | [betekənis] |

course (e.g., a French ~)	kursus	[kursus]
to sign up	inskryf	[inskrajf]
teacher	onderwyser	[ondərwajsər]

translation (process)	vertaling	[fertaliŋ]
translation (text, etc.)	vertaling	[fertaliŋ]
translator	vertaler	[fertalər]
interpreter	tolk	[tolk]

| polyglot | poliglot | [poliχlot] |
| memory | geheue | [χəhøə] |

MEALS. RESTAURANT

48. Table setting

spoon	**lepel**	[lepəl]
knife	**mes**	[mes]
fork	**vurk**	[furk]
cup (e.g., coffee ~)	**koppie**	[koppi]
plate (dinner ~)	**bord**	[bort]
saucer	**piering**	[piriŋ]
napkin (on table)	**servet**	[serfət]
toothpick	**tandestokkie**	[tandə·stokki]

49. Restaurant

restaurant	**restaurant**	[restɔurant]
coffee house	**koffiekroeg**	[koffi·kruχ]
pub, bar	**kroeg**	[kruχ]
tearoom	**teekamer**	[teə·kamər]
waiter	**kelner**	[kɛlnər]
waitress	**kelnerin**	[kɛlnərin]
bartender	**kroegman**	[kruχman]
menu	**spyskaart**	[spajs·kārt]
wine list	**wyn**	[vajn]
to book a table	**wynkaart**	[vajn·kārt]
course, dish	**gereg**	[χerəχ]
to order (meal)	**bestel**	[bestəl]
to make an order	**bestel**	[bestəl]
aperitif	**drankie**	[dranki]
appetizer	**voorgereg**	[foərχerəχ]
dessert	**nagereg**	[naχerəχ]
check	**rekening**	[rekəniŋ]
to pay the check	**die rekening betaal**	[di rekəniŋ betāl]
to give change	**kleingeld gee**	[klæjn·χɛlt χeə]
tip	**fooitjie**	[fojki]

50. Meals

food	**kos**	[kos]
to eat (vi, vt)	**eet**	[eət]
breakfast	**ontbyt**	[ontbajt]
to have breakfast	**ontbyt**	[ontbajt]
lunch	**middagete**	[middaχ·etə]
to have lunch	**gaan eet**	[χãn eət]
dinner	**aandete**	[ãndetə]
to have dinner	**aandete gebruik**	[ãndetə χebrœik]
appetite	**aptyt**	[aptajt]
Enjoy your meal!	**Smaaklike ete!**	[smãklikə etə!]
to open (~ a bottle)	**oopmaak**	[oəpmãk]
to spill (liquid)	**mors**	[mors]
to spill out (vi)	**mors**	[mors]
to boil (vi)	**kook**	[koək]
to boil (vt)	**kook**	[koək]
boiled (~ water)	**gekook**	[χekoək]
to chill, cool down (vt)	**laat afkoel**	[lãt afkul]
to chill (vi)	**afkoel**	[afkul]
taste, flavor	**smaak**	[smãk]
aftertaste	**nasmaak**	[nasmãk]
to slim down (lose weight)	**vermaer**	[fermaər]
diet	**dieet**	[diət]
vitamin	**vitamien**	[fitamin]
calorie	**kalorie**	[kalori]
vegetarian (n)	**vegetariër**	[feχetariɛr]
vegetarian (adj)	**vegetaries**	[feχetaris]
fats (nutrient)	**vette**	[fɛttə]
proteins	**proteïen**	[proteïen]
carbohydrates	**koolhidrate**	[koəlhidratə]
slice (of lemon, ham)	**snytjie**	[snajki]
piece (of cake, pie)	**stuk**	[stuk]
crumb (of bread, cake, etc.)	**krummel**	[krumməl]

51. Cooked dishes

course, dish	**gereg**	[χerəχ]
cuisine	**kookkuns**	[koək·kuns]
recipe	**resep**	[resep]

portion	**porsie**	[porsi]
salad	**slaai**	[slāi]
soup	**sop**	[sop]

clear soup (broth)	**helder sop**	[hɛldər sop]
sandwich (bread)	**toebroodjie**	[tubroədʒi]
fried eggs	**gabakte eiers**	[χabaktə æjers]

| hamburger (beefburger) | **hamburger** | [hamburχər] |
| beefsteak | **biefstuk** | [bifstuk] |

side dish	**sygereg**	[saj·χerəχ]
spaghetti	**spaghetti**	[spaχɛtti]
mashed potatoes	**kapokaartappels**	[kapok·ārtappəls]
pizza	**pizza**	[pizza]
porridge (oatmeal, etc.)	**pap**	[pap]
omelet	**omelet**	[oməlet]

boiled (e.g., ~ beef)	**gekook**	[χekoək]
smoked (adj)	**gerook**	[χeroək]
fried (adj)	**gebak**	[χebak]
dried (adj)	**gedroog**	[χedroəχ]
frozen (adj)	**gevries**	[χefris]
pickled (adj)	**gepiekel**	[χepikəl]

sweet (sugary)	**soet**	[sut]
salty (adj)	**sout**	[sæut]
cold (adj)	**koud**	[kæut]
hot (adj)	**warm**	[varm]
bitter (adj)	**bitter**	[bittər]
tasty (adj)	**smaaklik**	[smāklik]

to cook in boiling water	**kook in water**	[koək in vatər]
to cook (dinner)	**kook**	[koək]
to fry (vt)	**braai**	[braj]
to heat up (food)	**opwarm**	[opwarm]

to salt (vt)	**sout**	[sæut]
to pepper (vt)	**peper**	[pepər]
to grate (vt)	**rasp**	[rasp]
peel (n)	**skil**	[skil]
to peel (vt)	**skil**	[skil]

52. Food

meat	**vleis**	[flæjs]
chicken	**hoender**	[hundər]
Rock Cornish hen (poussin)	**braaikuiken**	[brāj·koəiken]
duck	**eend**	[eent]

goose	**gans**	[χaŋs]
game	**wild**	[vilt]
turkey	**kalkoen**	[kalkun]
pork	**varkvleis**	[fark·flæjs]
veal	**kalfsvleis**	[kalfs·flæjs]
lamb	**lamsvleis**	[lams·flæjs]
beef	**beesvleis**	[beəs·flæjs]
rabbit	**konynvleis**	[konajn·flæjs]
sausage (bologna, pepperoni, etc.)	**wors**	[vors]
vienna sausage (frankfurter)	**Weense worsie**	[veɛŋsə vorsi]
bacon	**spek**	[spek]
ham	**ham**	[ham]
gammon	**gerookte ham**	[χeroəktə ham]
pâté	**patee**	[pateə]
liver	**lewer**	[levər]
hamburger (ground beef)	**maalvleis**	[māl·flæjs]
tongue	**tong**	[toŋ]
egg	**eier**	[æjer]
eggs	**eiers**	[æjers]
egg white	**eierwit**	[æjer·wit]
egg yolk	**dooier**	[dojer]
fish	**vis**	[fis]
seafood	**seekos**	[seə·kos]
crustaceans	**skaaldiere**	[skāldirə]
caviar	**kaviaar**	[kafiār]
crab	**krab**	[krap]
shrimp	**garnaal**	[χarnāl]
oyster	**oester**	[ustər]
spiny lobster	**seekreef**	[seə·kreəf]
octopus	**seekat**	[seə·kat]
squid	**pylinkvis**	[pajl·inkfis]
sturgeon	**steur**	[støər]
salmon	**salm**	[salm]
halibut	**heilbot**	[hæjlbot]
cod	**kabeljou**	[kabeljæʊ]
mackerel	**makriel**	[makril]
tuna	**tuna**	[tuna]
eel	**paling**	[paliŋ]
trout	**forel**	[forəl]
sardine	**sardyn**	[sardajn]
pike	**varswatersnoek**	[farswatər·snuk]

herring	haring	[hariŋ]
bread	brood	[broət]
cheese	kaas	[kās]
sugar	suiker	[sœikər]
salt	sout	[sæʋt]

rice	rys	[rajs]
pasta (macaroni)	pasta	[pasta]
noodles	noedels	[nudɛls]

butter	botter	[bottər]
vegetable oil	plantaardige olie	[plantãrdiχə oli]
sunflower oil	sonblomolie	[sonblom·oli]
margarine	margarien	[marχarin]

| olives | olywe | [olajvə] |
| olive oil | olyfolie | [olajf·oli] |

milk	melk	[mɛlk]
condensed milk	kondensmelk	[kondɛŋs·mɛlk]
yogurt	jogurt	[joχurt]
sour cream	suurroom	[sɪr·roəm]
cream (of milk)	room	[roəm]

| mayonnaise | mayonnaise | [majonɛs] |
| buttercream | crème | [krɛm] |

cereal grains (wheat, etc.)	ontbytgraan	[ontbajt·χrān]
flour	meelblom	[meəl·blom]
canned food	blikkieskos	[blikkis·kos]

cornflakes	mielievlokkies	[mili·flokkis]
honey	heuning	[høəniŋ]
jam	konfyt	[konfajt]
chewing gum	kougom	[kæʋχom]

53. Drinks

water	water	[vatər]
drinking water	drinkwater	[drink·vatər]
mineral water	mineraalwater	[minerāl·vatər]

still (adj)	sonder gas	[sondər χas]
carbonated (adj)	soda-	[soda-]
sparkling (adj)	bruis-	[brœis-]
ice	ys	[ajs]
with ice	met ys	[met ajs]

| non-alcoholic (adj) | nie-alkoholies | [ni-alkoholis] |
| soft drink | koeldrank | [kul·drank] |

| refreshing drink | verfrissende drank | [ferfrissendə drank] |
| lemonade | limonade | [limonadə] |

liquors	likeure	[likøərə]
wine	wyn	[vajn]
white wine	witwyn	[vit·vajn]
red wine	rooiwyn	[roj·vajn]

liqueur	likeur	[likøər]
champagne	sjampanje	[ʃampanje]
vermouth	vermoet	[fermut]

whiskey	whisky	[vhiskaj]
vodka	vodka	[fodka]
gin	jenever	[jenefər]
cognac	brandewyn	[brandə·vajn]
rum	rum	[rum]

coffee	koffie	[koffi]
black coffee	swart koffie	[swart koffi]
coffee with milk	koffie met melk	[koffi met melk]
cappuccino	capuccino	[kaputʃino]
instant coffee	poeierkoffie	[pujer·koffi]

milk	melk	[melk]
cocktail	mengeldrankie	[menχəl·dranki]
milkshake	melkskommel	[melk·skomməl]

juice	sap	[sap]
tomato juice	tamatiesap	[tamati·sap]
orange juice	lemoensap	[lemoən·sap]
freshly squeezed juice	vars geparste sap	[fars χeparstə sap]

beer	bier	[bir]
light beer	ligte bier	[liχtə bir]
dark beer	donker bier	[donkər bir]

tea	tee	[teə]
black tea	swart tee	[swart teə]
green tea	groen tee	[χrun teə]

54. Vegetables

| vegetables | groente | [χruntə] |
| greens | groente | [χruntə] |

tomato	tamatie	[tamati]
cucumber	komkommer	[komkommər]
carrot	wortel	[vortəl]
potato	aartappel	[ãrtappəl]

| onion | ui | [œi] |
| garlic | **knoffel** | [knoffəl] |

cabbage	**kool**	[koəl]
cauliflower	**blomkool**	[blom·koəl]
Brussels sprouts	**Brusselspruite**	[brussɛl·sprœitə]
broccoli	**broccoli**	[brokoli]

beetroot	**beet**	[beət]
eggplant	**eiervrug**	[æjerfruχ]
zucchini	**vingerskorsie**	[fiŋər·skorsi]
pumpkin	**pampoen**	[pampun]
turnip	**raap**	[rãp]

parsley	**pietersielie**	[pitərsili]
dill	**dille**	[dillə]
lettuce	**slaai**	[slãi]
celery	**seldery**	[selderaj]
asparagus	**aspersie**	[aspersi]
spinach	**spinasie**	[spinasi]

pea	**ertjie**	[ɛrki]
beans	**boontjies**	[boənkis]
corn (maize)	**mielie**	[mili]
kidney bean	**nierboontjie**	[nir·boənki]

bell pepper	**paprika**	[paprika]
radish	**radys**	[radajs]
artichoke	**artisjok**	[artiʃok]

55. Fruits. Nuts

fruit	**vrugte**	[fruχtə]
apple	**appel**	[appəl]
pear	**peer**	[peər]
lemon	**suurlemoen**	[sɪr·lemun]
orange	**lemoen**	[lemun]
strawberry (garden ~)	**aarbei**	[ãrbæj]

mandarin	**nartjie**	[narki]
plum	**pruim**	[prœim]
peach	**perske**	[perskə]
apricot	**appelkoos**	[appɛlkoəs]
raspberry	**framboos**	[framboəs]
pineapple	**pynappel**	[pajnappəl]

banana	**piesang**	[pisaŋ]
watermelon	**waatlemoen**	[vãtlemun]
grape	**druif**	[drœif]
cherry	**kersie**	[kersi]

sour cherry	suurkersie	[sɪr·kersi]
sweet cherry	soetkersie	[sut·kersi]
melon	spanspek	[spaŋspek]

grapefruit	pomelo	[pomelo]
avocado	avokado	[afokado]
papaya	papaja	[papaja]
mango	mango	[manχo]
pomegranate	granaat	[χranãt]

redcurrant	rooi aalbessie	[roj ãlbɛssi]
blackcurrant	swartbessie	[swartbɛssi]
gooseberry	appelliefie	[appɛllifi]
bilberry	bosbessie	[bosbɛssi]
blackberry	braambessie	[brãmbɛssi]

raisin	rosyntjie	[rosajnki]
fig	vy	[faj]
date	dadel	[dadəl]

peanut	grondboontjie	[χront·boənki]
almond	amandel	[amandəl]
walnut	okkerneut	[okkər·nøət]
hazelnut	haselneut	[hasɛl·nøət]
coconut	klapper	[klappər]
pistachios	pistachio	[pistatʃio]

56. Bread. Candy

bakers' confectionery (pastry)	soet gebak	[sut χebak]
bread	brood	[broət]
cookies	koekies	[kukis]

chocolate (n)	sjokolade	[ʃokoladə]
chocolate (as adj)	sjokolade	[ʃokoladə]
candy (wrapped)	lekkers	[lɛkkərs]

| cake (e.g., cupcake) | koek | [kuk] |
| cake (e.g., birthday ~) | koek | [kuk] |

| pie (e.g., apple ~) | pastei | [pastæj] |
| filling (for cake, pie) | vulsel | [fulsəl] |

| jam (whole fruit jam) | konfyt | [konfajt] |
| marmalade | marmelade | [marmeladə] |

waffles	wafels	[vafɛls]
ice-cream	roomys	[roəm·ajs]
pudding	poeding	[pudiŋ]

57. Spices

salt	**sout**	[sæʊt]
salty (adj)	**sout**	[sæʊt]
to salt (vt)	**sout**	[sæʊt]
black pepper	**swart peper**	[swart pepər]
red pepper (milled ~)	**rooi peper**	[roj pepər]
mustard	**mosterd**	[mostert]
horseradish	**peperwortel**	[peper·wortəl]
condiment	**smaakmiddel**	[smāk·middəl]
spice	**spesery**	[spesəraj]
sauce	**sous**	[sæʊs]
vinegar	**asyn**	[asajn]
anise	**anys**	[anajs]
basil	**basilikum**	[basilikum]
cloves	**naeltjies**	[naɛlkis]
ginger	**gemmer**	[χɛmmər]
coriander	**koljander**	[koljandər]
cinnamon	**kaneel**	[kaneəl]
sesame	**sesamsaad**	[sesam·sāt]
bay leaf	**lourierblaar**	[læʊrir·blār]
paprika	**paprika**	[paprika]
caraway	**komynsaad**	[komajnsāt]
saffron	**saffraan**	[saffrān]

PERSONAL INFORMATION. FAMILY

58. Personal information. Forms

name (first name)	**voornaam**	[foǝrnãm]
surname (last name)	**van**	[fan]
date of birth	**geboortedatum**	[χeboǝrtǝ·datum]
place of birth	**geboorteplek**	[χeboǝrtǝ·plek]
nationality	**nasionaliteit**	[naʃionalitæjt]
place of residence	**woonplek**	[voǝn·plek]
country	**land**	[lant]
profession (occupation)	**beroep**	[berup]
gender, sex	**geslag**	[χeslaχ]
height	**lengte**	[leɳtǝ]
weight	**gewig**	[χevǝχ]

59. Family members. Relatives

mother	**moeder**	[mudǝr]
father	**vader**	[fadǝr]
son	**seun**	[søǝn]
daughter	**dogter**	[doχtǝr]
younger daughter	**jonger dogter**	[joɳǝr doχtǝr]
younger son	**jonger seun**	[joɳǝr søǝn]
eldest daughter	**oudste dogter**	[æʊdstǝ doχtǝr]
eldest son	**oudste seun**	[æʊdstǝ søǝn]
brother	**broer**	[brur]
elder brother	**ouer broer**	[æʊer brur]
younger brother	**jonger broer**	[joɳǝr brur]
sister	**suster**	[sustǝr]
elder sister	**ouer suster**	[æʊer sustǝr]
younger sister	**jonger suster**	[joɳǝr sustǝr]
cousin (masc.)	**neef**	[neǝf]
cousin (fem.)	**neef**	[neǝf]
mom, mommy	**ma**	[ma]
dad, daddy	**pa**	[pa]
parents	**ouers**	[æʊers]
child	**kind**	[kint]
children	**kinders**	[kindǝrs]

grandmother	**ouma**	[æʊma]
grandfather	**oupa**	[æʊpa]
grandson	**kleinseun**	[klæjn·søən]
granddaughter	**kleindogter**	[klæjn·doχtər]
grandchildren	**kleinkinders**	[klæjn·kindərs]
uncle	**oom**	[oəm]
aunt	**tante**	[tantə]
nephew	**neef**	[neəf]
niece	**nig**	[niχ]
mother-in-law (wife's mother)	**skoonma**	[skoən·ma]
father-in-law (husband's father)	**skoonpa**	[skoən·pa]
son-in-law (daughter's husband)	**skoonseun**	[skoən·søən]
stepmother	**stiefma**	[stifma]
stepfather	**stiefpa**	[stifpa]
infant	**baba**	[baba]
baby (infant)	**baba**	[baba]
little boy, kid	**seuntjie**	[søənki]
wife	**vrou**	[fræʊ]
husband	**man**	[man]
spouse (husband)	**eggenoot**	[ɛχχenoət]
spouse (wife)	**eggenote**	[ɛχχenotə]
married (masc.)	**getroud**	[χetræʊt]
married (fem.)	**getroud**	[χetræʊt]
single (unmarried)	**ongetroud**	[onχetræʊt]
bachelor	**vrygesel**	[frajχesəl]
divorced (masc.)	**geskei**	[χeskæj]
widow	**weduwee**	[veduveə]
widower	**wedunaar**	[vedunār]
relative	**familielid**	[famililit]
close relative	**na familie**	[na famili]
distant relative	**ver familie**	[fer famili]
relatives	**familielede**	[famililedə]
orphan (boy or girl)	**weeskind**	[veəskint]
guardian (of a minor)	**voog**	[foəχ]
to adopt (a boy)	**aanneem**	[ānneəm]
to adopt (a girl)	**aanneem**	[ānneəm]

60. Friends. Coworkers

| friend (masc.) | **vriend** | [frint] |
| friend (fem.) | **vriendin** | [frindin] |

friendship	**vriendskap**	[frindskap]
to be friends	**bevriend wees**	[befrint veəs]
buddy (masc.)	**maat**	[māt]
buddy (fem.)	**vriendin**	[frindin]
partner	**maat**	[māt]
chief (boss)	**baas**	[bās]
superior (n)	**baas**	[bās]
owner, proprietor	**eienaar**	[æjenār]
subordinate (n)	**ondergeskikte**	[ondərχeskiktə]
colleague	**kollega**	[kolleχa]
acquaintance (person)	**kennis**	[kɛnnis]
fellow traveler	**medereisiger**	[medə·ræjsiχər]
classmate	**klasmaat**	[klas·māt]
neighbor (masc.)	**buurman**	[bɪrman]
neighbor (fem.)	**buurvrou**	[bɪrfræʊ]
neighbors	**bure**	[burə]

HUMAN BODY. MEDICINE

61. Head

head	**kop**	[kɔp]
face	**gesig**	[χesəχ]
nose	**neus**	[nøəs]
mouth	**mond**	[mont]
eye	**oog**	[oəχ]
eyes	**oë**	[oɛ]
pupil	**pupil**	[pupil]
eyebrow	**wenkbrou**	[vɛnk·bræʊ]
eyelash	**ooghaar**	[oəχ·hãr]
eyelid	**ooglid**	[oəχ·lit]
tongue	**tong**	[tɔŋ]
tooth	**tand**	[tant]
lips	**lippe**	[lippə]
cheekbones	**wangbene**	[vaŋ·benə]
gum	**tandvleis**	[tand·flæjs]
palate	**verhemelte**	[fer·hemɛltə]
nostrils	**neusgate**	[nøəsχatə]
chin	**ken**	[ken]
jaw	**kakebeen**	[kakebeən]
cheek	**wang**	[vaŋ]
forehead	**voorhoof**	[foərhoəf]
temple	**slaap**	[slãp]
ear	**oor**	[oər]
back of the head	**agterkop**	[aχtərkop]
neck	**nek**	[nek]
throat	**keel**	[keəl]
hair	**haar**	[hãr]
hairstyle	**kapsel**	[kapsəl]
haircut	**haarstyl**	[hãrstajl]
wig	**pruik**	[prœik]
mustache	**snor**	[snor]
beard	**baard**	[bãrt]
to have (a beard, etc.)	**dra**	[dra]
braid	**vlegsel**	[fleχsəl]
sideburns	**bakkebaarde**	[bakkəbãrdə]
red-haired (adj)	**rooiharig**	[roj·harəχ]

gray (hair)	**grys**	[χrajs]
bald (adj)	**kaal**	[kãl]
bald patch	**kaal plek**	[kãl plek]

| ponytail | **poniestert** | [poni·stert] |
| bangs | **gordyntjiekapsel** | [χordajnki·kapsəl] |

62. Human body

| hand | **hand** | [hant] |
| arm | **arm** | [arm] |

finger	**vinger**	[fiŋər]
toe	**toon**	[toən]
thumb	**duim**	[dœim]
little finger	**pinkie**	[pinki]
nail	**nael**	[naəl]

fist	**vuis**	[fœis]
palm	**palm**	[palm]
wrist	**pols**	[pols]
forearm	**voorarm**	[foərarm]
elbow	**elmboog**	[ɛlmboəχ]
shoulder	**skouer**	[skæʋər]

leg	**been**	[beən]
foot	**voet**	[fut]
knee	**knie**	[kni]
calf (part of leg)	**kuit**	[kœit]
hip	**heup**	[høəp]
heel	**hakskeen**	[hak·skeən]

body	**liggaam**	[liχχãm]
stomach	**maag**	[mãχ]
chest	**bors**	[bors]
breast	**bors**	[bors]
flank	**sy**	[saj]
back	**rug**	[ruχ]
lower back	**lae rug**	[laə ruχ]
waist	**middel**	[middəl]

navel (belly button)	**naeltjie**	[naɛlki]
buttocks	**boude**	[bæʋdə]
bottom	**sitvlak**	[sitflak]

beauty mark	**moesie**	[musi]
birthmark (café au lait spot)	**moedervlek**	[mudər·flek]
tattoo	**tatoe**	[tatu]
scar	**litteken**	[littekən]

63. Diseases

sickness	**siekte**	[siktə]
to be sick	**siek wees**	[sik veəs]
health	**gesondheid**	[χesonthæjt]
runny nose (coryza)	**loopneus**	[loəpnøəs]
tonsillitis	**keelontsteking**	[keəl·ontstekiŋ]
cold (illness)	**verkoue**	[ferkæʊə]
bronchitis	**bronchitis**	[bronχitis]
pneumonia	**longontsteking**	[loŋ·ontstekiŋ]
flu, influenza	**griep**	[χrip]
nearsighted (adj)	**bysiende**	[bajsində]
farsighted (adj)	**versiende**	[fersində]
strabismus (crossed eyes)	**skeelheid**	[skeəlhæjt]
cross-eyed (adj)	**skeel**	[skeəl]
cataract	**katarak**	[katarak]
glaucoma	**gloukoom**	[χlæʊkoəm]
stroke	**beroerte**	[berurtə]
heart attack	**hartaanval**	[hart·ānfal]
myocardial infarction	**hartinfark**	[hart·infark]
paralysis	**verlamming**	[ferlammiŋ]
to paralyze (vt)	**verlam**	[ferlam]
allergy	**allergie**	[allerχi]
asthma	**asma**	[asma]
diabetes	**suikersiekte**	[sœikər·siktə]
toothache	**tandpyn**	[tand·pajn]
caries	**tandbederf**	[tand·bederf]
diarrhea	**diarree**	[diarreə]
constipation	**hardlywigheid**	[hardlajviχæjt]
stomach upset	**maagongesteldheid**	[māχ·oŋəstɛldhæjt]
food poisoning	**voedselvergiftiging**	[fudsəl·ferχiftəχiŋ]
to get food poisoning	**voedselvergiftiging kry**	[fudsəl·ferχiftəχiŋ kraj]
arthritis	**artritis**	[artritis]
rickets	**Engelse siekte**	[ɛŋəlsə siktə]
rheumatism	**reumatiek**	[røəmatik]
atherosclerosis	**artrosklerose**	[artrosklerosə]
gastritis	**maagontsteking**	[māχ·ontstekiŋ]
appendicitis	**blindedermontsteking**	[blindəderm·ontstekiŋ]
cholecystitis	**galblaasontsteking**	[χalblās·ontstekiŋ]
ulcer	**maagsweer**	[māχsweər]
measles	**masels**	[masɛls]
rubella (German measles)	**Duitse masels**	[dœitsə masɛls]

jaundice	**geelsug**	[χeəlsuχ]
hepatitis	**hepatitis**	[hepatitis]
schizophrenia	**skisofrenie**	[skisofreni]
rabies (hydrophobia)	**hondsdolheid**	[hondsdolhæjt]
neurosis	**neurose**	[nøərosə]
concussion	**harsingskudding**	[harsiŋ·skuddiŋ]
cancer	**kanker**	[kankər]
sclerosis	**sklerose**	[sklerosə]
multiple sclerosis	**veelvuldige sklerose**	[feəlfuldiχə sklerosə]
alcoholism	**alkoholisme**	[alkoholismə]
alcoholic (n)	**alkoholikus**	[alkoholikus]
syphilis	**sifilis**	[sifilis]
AIDS	**VIGS**	[vigs]
tumor	**tumor**	[tumor]
malignant (adj)	**kwaadaardig**	[kwãdãrdəχ]
benign (adj)	**goedaardig**	[χudãrdəχ]
fever	**koors**	[koərs]
malaria	**malaria**	[malaria]
gangrene	**gangreen**	[χanχreən]
seasickness	**seesiekte**	[seə·siktə]
epilepsy	**epilepsie**	[ɛpilepsi]
epidemic	**epidemie**	[ɛpidemi]
typhus	**tifus**	[tifus]
tuberculosis	**tuberkulose**	[tuberkulosə]
cholera	**cholera**	[χolera]
plague (bubonic ~)	**pes**	[pes]

64. Symptoms. Treatments. Part 1

symptom	**simptoom**	[simptoəm]
temperature	**temperatuur**	[temperatɪr]
high temperature (fever)	**koors**	[koərs]
pulse	**polsslag**	[pols·slaχ]
dizziness (vertigo)	**duiseligheid**	[dœiseliχæjt]
hot (adj)	**warm**	[varm]
shivering	**koue rillings**	[kæʊə rilliŋs]
pale (e.g., ~ face)	**bleek**	[bleək]
cough	**hoes**	[hus]
to cough (vi)	**hoes**	[hus]
to sneeze (vi)	**nies**	[nis]
faint	**floute**	[flæʊtə]
to faint (vi)	**flou word**	[flæʊ vort]

bruise (hématome)	blou kol	[blæʊ kol]
bump (lump)	knop	[knop]
to bang (bump)	stamp	[stamp]
contusion (bruise)	besering	[beseriŋ]

to limp (vi)	hink	[hink]
dislocation	ontwrigting	[ontwriχtiŋ]
to dislocate (vt)	ontwrig	[ontwrəχ]
fracture	breuk	[brøək]
to have a fracture	n breuk hè	[n brøək hɛ:]

cut (e.g., paper ~)	sny	[snaj]
to cut oneself	jouself sny	[jæʊsɛlf snaj]
bleeding	bloeding	[bludiŋ]

| burn (injury) | brandwond | [brant·vont] |
| to get burned | jouself brand | [jæʊsɛlf brant] |

to prick (vt)	prik	[prik]
to prick oneself	jouself prik	[jæʊsɛlf prik]
to injure (vt)	seermaak	[seərmāk]
injury	besering	[beseriŋ]
wound	wond	[vont]
trauma	trauma	[trɔuma]

to be delirious	yl	[ajl]
to stutter (vi)	stotter	[stottər]
sunstroke	sonsteek	[sɔŋ·steək]

65. Symptoms. Treatments. Part 2

| pain, ache | pyn | [pajn] |
| splinter (in foot, etc.) | splinter | [splintər] |

sweat (perspiration)	sweet	[sweət]
to sweat (perspire)	sweet	[sweət]
vomiting	braak	[brāk]
convulsions	stuiptrekkings	[stœip·trɛkkiŋs]

pregnant (adj)	swanger	[swaŋər]
to be born	gebore word	[χeborə vort]
delivery, labor	geboorte	[χeboərtə]
to deliver (~ a baby)	baar	[bār]
abortion	aborsie	[aborsi]

breathing, respiration	asemhaling	[asemhaliŋ]
in-breath (inhalation)	inaseming	[inasemiŋ]
out-breath (exhalation)	uitaseming	[œitasemiŋ]
to exhale (breathe out)	uitasem	[œitasem]
to inhale (vi)	inasem	[inasem]

disabled person	**invalide**	[infalidə]
cripple	**kreupel**	[krøəpəl]
drug addict	**dwelmslaaf**	[dwɛlm·slāf]
deaf (adj)	**doof**	[doəf]
mute (adj)	**stom**	[stom]
deaf mute (adj)	**doofstom**	[doəf·stom]
mad, insane (adj)	**swaksinnig**	[swaksinnəx]
madman	**kranksinnige**	[kranksinnixə]
(demented person)		
madwoman	**kranksinnige**	[kranksinnixə]
to go insane	**kranksinnig word**	[kranksinnəx vort]
gene	**geen**	[xeən]
immunity	**immuniteit**	[immunitæjt]
hereditary (adj)	**erflik**	[ɛrflik]
congenital (adj)	**aangebore**	[ānxəborə]
virus	**virus**	[firus]
microbe	**mikrobe**	[mikrobə]
bacterium	**bakterie**	[bakteri]
infection	**infeksie**	[infeksi]

66. Symptoms. Treatments. Part 3

hospital	**hospitaal**	[hospitāl]
patient	**pasiënt**	[pasiɛnt]
diagnosis	**diagnose**	[diaxnosə]
cure	**genesing**	[xenesiŋ]
medical treatment	**mediese behandeling**	[medisə behandəliŋ]
to get treatment	**behandeling kry**	[behandəliŋ kraj]
to treat (~ a patient)	**behandel**	[behandəl]
to nurse (look after)	**versorg**	[fersorx]
care (nursing ~)	**versorging**	[fersorxiŋ]
operation, surgery	**operasie**	[operasi]
to bandage (head, limb)	**verbind**	[ferbint]
bandaging	**verband**	[ferbant]
vaccination	**inenting**	[inɛntiŋ]
to vaccinate (vt)	**inent**	[inɛnt]
injection, shot	**inspuiting**	[inspœitiŋ]
attack	**aanval**	[ānfal]
amputation	**amputasie**	[amputasi]
to amputate (vt)	**amputeer**	[amputeər]
coma	**koma**	[koma]
intensive care	**intensiewe sorg**	[intɛnsivə sorx]

to recover (~ from flu)	herstel	[herstəl]
condition (patient's ~)	kondisie	[kondisi]
consciousness	bewussyn	[bevussajn]
memory (faculty)	geheue	[χəhøə]

to pull out (tooth)	trek	[trek]
filling	vulsel	[fulsəl]
to fill (a tooth)	vul	[ful]

| hypnosis | hipnose | [hipnosə] |
| to hypnotize (vt) | hipnotiseer | [hipnotiseər] |

67. Medicine. Drugs. Accessories

medicine, drug	medisyn	[medisajn]
remedy	geneesmiddel	[χenees·middəl]
to prescribe (vt)	voorskryf	[foərskrajf]
prescription	voorskrif	[foərskrif]

tablet, pill	pil	[pil]
ointment	salf	[salf]
ampule	ampul	[ampul]
mixture	mengsel	[meŋsəl]
syrup	stroop	[stroəp]
pill	pil	[pil]
powder	poeier	[pujer]

gauze bandage	verband	[ferbant]
cotton wool	watte	[vattə]
iodine	iodium	[iodium]

Band-Aid	pleister	[plæjstər]
eyedropper	oogdrupper	[oəχ·druppər]
thermometer	termometer	[termometər]
syringe	spuitnaald	[spœit·nãlt]

| wheelchair | rolstoel | [rol·stul] |
| crutches | krukke | [krukkə] |

painkiller	pynstiller	[pajn·stillər]
laxative	lakseermiddel	[lakseər·middəl]
spirits (ethanol)	spiritus	[spiritus]
medicinal herbs	geneeskragtige kruie	[χenees·kraχtiχə krœeiə]
herbal (~ tea)	kruie-	[krœie-]

APARTMENT

68. Apartment

apartment	**woonstel**	[voəŋstəl]
room	**kamer**	[kamər]
bedroom	**slaapkamer**	[slāp·kamər]
dining room	**eetkamer**	[eət·kamər]
living room	**sitkamer**	[sit·kamər]
study (home office)	**studeerkamer**	[studeər·kamər]
entry room	**ingangsportaal**	[inχaŋs·portāl]
bathroom (room with a bath or shower)	**badkamer**	[bad·kamər]
half bath	**toilet**	[tojlet]
ceiling	**plafon**	[plafon]
floor	**vloer**	[flur]
corner	**hoek**	[huk]

69. Furniture. Interior

furniture	**meubels**	[møəbɛls]
table	**tafel**	[tafel]
chair	**stoel**	[stul]
bed	**bed**	[bet]
couch, sofa	**rusbank**	[rusbank]
armchair	**gemakstoel**	[χemak·stul]
bookcase	**boekkas**	[buk·kas]
shelf	**rak**	[rak]
wardrobe	**klerekas**	[klerə·kas]
coat rack (wall-mounted ~)	**kapstok**	[kapstok]
coat stand	**kapstok**	[kapstok]
bureau, dresser	**laaikas**	[lājkas]
coffee table	**koffietafel**	[koffi·tafəl]
mirror	**spieêl**	[spiɛl]
carpet	**mat**	[mat]
rug, small carpet	**matjie**	[maki]
fireplace	**vuurherd**	[fɪr·hert]
candle	**kers**	[kers]

candlestick	**kandelaar**	[kandelãr]
drapes	**gordyne**	[χordajnə]
wallpaper	**muurpapier**	[mɪr·papir]
blinds (jalousie)	**blindings**	[blindiŋs]

table lamp	**tafellamp**	[tafel·lamp]
wall lamp (sconce)	**muurlamp**	[mɪr·lamp]
floor lamp	**staanlamp**	[stãn·lamp]
chandelier	**kroonlugter**	[kroən·luχtər]

leg (of chair, table)	**poot**	[poət]
armrest	**armleuning**	[arm·løəniŋ]
back (backrest)	**rugleuning**	[ruχ·løəniŋ]
drawer	**laai**	[lãi]

70. Bedding

bedclothes	**beddegoed**	[beddə·χut]
pillow	**kussing**	[kussiŋ]
pillowcase	**kussingsloop**	[kussiŋ·sloəp]
duvet, comforter	**duvet**	[dufet]
sheet	**laken**	[laken]
bedspread	**bedsprei**	[bed·spræj]

71. Kitchen

kitchen	**kombuis**	[kombœis]
gas	**gas**	[χas]
gas stove (range)	**gasstoof**	[χas·stoəf]
electric stove	**elektriese stoof**	[elektrisə stoəf]
oven	**oond**	[oent]
microwave oven	**mikrogolfoond**	[mikroχolf·oent]

refrigerator	**yskas**	[ajs·kas]
freezer	**vrieskas**	[friskas]
dishwasher	**skottelgoedwasser**	[skottɛlχud·wassər]

meat grinder	**vleismeul**	[flæjs·møəl]
juicer	**versapper**	[fersappər]
toaster	**broodrooster**	[broəd·roəstər]
mixer	**menger**	[meŋər]

coffee machine	**koffiemasjien**	[koffi·maʃin]
coffee pot	**koffiepot**	[koffi·pot]
coffee grinder	**koffiemeul**	[koffi·møəl]

| kettle | **fluitketel** | [flœit·ketəl] |
| teapot | **teepot** | [teə·pot] |

lid	deksel	[deksəl]
tea strainer	teesiffie	[teə·siffi]
spoon	lepel	[lepəl]
teaspoon	teelepeltjie	[teə·lepəlki]
soup spoon	soplepel	[sop·lepəl]
fork	vurk	[furk]
knife	mes	[mes]
tableware (dishes)	tafelgerei	[tafel·χeræj]
plate (dinner ~)	bord	[bort]
saucer	piering	[piriŋ]
shot glass	likeurglas	[likøər·χlas]
glass (tumbler)	glas	[χlas]
cup	koppie	[koppi]
sugar bowl	suikerpot	[sœikər·pot]
salt shaker	soutvaatjie	[sæʊt·fāki]
pepper shaker	pepervaatjie	[pepər·fāki]
butter dish	botterbakkie	[bottər·bakki]
stock pot (soup pot)	soppot	[sop·pot]
frying pan (skillet)	braaipan	[brāj·pan]
ladle	opskeplepel	[opskep·lepəl]
colander	vergiet	[ferχit]
tray (serving ~)	skinkbord	[skink·bort]
bottle	bottel	[bottəl]
jar (glass)	fles	[fles]
can	blikkie	[blikki]
bottle opener	botteloopmaker	[bottəl·oəpmakər]
can opener	blikoopmaker	[blik·oəpmakər]
corkscrew	kurktrekker	[kurk·trɛkkər]
filter	filter	[filtər]
to filter (vt)	filter	[filtər]
trash, garbage (food waste, etc.)	vullis	[fullis]
trash can (kitchen ~)	vullisbak	[fullis·bak]

72. Bathroom

bathroom	badkamer	[bad·kamər]
water	water	[vatər]
faucet	kraan	[krān]
hot water	warme water	[varmə vatər]
cold water	koue water	[kæʊə vatər]
toothpaste	tandepasta	[tandə·pasta]

| to brush one's teeth | **tande borsel** | [tandə borsəl] |
| toothbrush | **tandeborsel** | [tandə·borsəl] |

to shave (vi)	**skeer**	[skeər]
shaving foam	**skeerroom**	[skeər·roəm]
razor	**skeermes**	[skeər·mes]

to wash (one's hands, etc.)	**was**	[vas]
to take a bath	**bad**	[bat]
shower	**stort**	[stort]
to take a shower	**stort**	[stort]

bathtub	**bad**	[bat]
toilet (toilet bowl)	**toilet**	[tojlet]
sink (washbasin)	**wasbak**	[vas·bak]

| soap | **seep** | [seəp] |
| soap dish | **seepbakkie** | [seəp·bakki] |

sponge	**spons**	[spoŋs]
shampoo	**sjampoe**	[ʃampu]
towel	**handdoek**	[handduk]
bathrobe	**badjas**	[batjas]

laundry (process)	**was**	[vas]
washing machine	**wasmasjien**	[vas·maʃin]
to do the laundry	**die wasgoed was**	[di vasχut vas]
laundry detergent	**waspoeier**	[vas·pujer]

73. Household appliances

TV set	**TV-stel**	[te·fe-stəl]
tape recorder	**bandspeler**	[band·spelər]
VCR (video recorder)	**videomasjien**	[video·maʃin]
radio	**radio**	[radio]
player (CD, MP3, etc.)	**speler**	[spelər]

video projector	**videoprojektor**	[video·projektor]
home movie theater	**tuisfliekteater**	[tœis·flik·teatər]
DVD player	**DVD-speler**	[de·fe·de-spelər]
amplifier	**versterker**	[fersterkər]
video game console	**videokonsole**	[video·kɔŋsolə]

video camera	**videokamera**	[video·kamera]
camera (photo)	**kamera**	[kamera]
digital camera	**digitale kamera**	[diχitalə kamera]

vacuum cleaner	**stofsuier**	[stof·sœiər]
iron (e.g., steam ~)	**strykyster**	[strajk·ajstər]
ironing board	**strykplank**	[strajk·plank]

telephone	**telefoon**	[telefoən]
cell phone	**selfoon**	[sɛlfoən]
typewriter	**tikmasjien**	[tik·maʃin]
sewing machine	**naaimasjien**	[naj·maʃin]

microphone	**mikrofoon**	[mikrofoən]
headphones	**koptelefoon**	[kop·telefoən]
remote control (TV)	**afstandsbeheer**	[afstands·beheər]

CD, compact disc	**CD**	[se·de]
cassette, tape	**kasset**	[kasset]
vinyl record	**plaat**	[plãt]

THE EARTH. WEATHER

74. Outer space

space	**kosmos**	[kosmos]
space (as adj)	**kosmies**	[kosmis]
outer space	**buitenste ruimte**	[bœitɛŋstə rajmtə]
world	**wêreld**	[værɛlt]
universe	**heelal**	[heəlal]
galaxy	**sterrestelsel**	[sterrə·stɛlsəl]
star	**ster**	[ster]
constellation	**sterrebeeld**	[sterrə·beəlt]
planet	**planeet**	[planeət]
satellite	**satelliet**	[satɛllit]
meteorite	**meteoriet**	[meteorit]
comet	**komeet**	[komeət]
asteroid	**asteroïed**	[asteroïət]
orbit	**baan**	[bān]
to revolve	**draai**	[drāi]
(~ around the Earth)		
atmosphere	**atmosfeer**	[atmosfeər]
the Sun	**die Son**	[di son]
solar system	**sonnestelsel**	[sonnə·stɛlsəl]
solar eclipse	**sonsverduistering**	[soŋs·ferdœisteriŋ]
the Earth	**die Aarde**	[di ārdə]
the Moon	**die Maan**	[di mān]
Mars	**Mars**	[mars]
Venus	**Venus**	[fenus]
Jupiter	**Jupiter**	[jupitər]
Saturn	**Saturnus**	[saturnus]
Mercury	**Mercurius**	[merkurius]
Uranus	**Uranus**	[uranus]
Neptune	**Neptunus**	[neptunus]
Pluto	**Pluto**	[pluto]
Milky Way	**Melkweg**	[melk·weχ]
Great Bear (Ursa Major)	**Groot Beer**	[χroet beər]
North Star	**Poolster**	[poəl·stər]

Martian	marsbewoner	[mars·bevonər]
extraterrestrial (n)	buiteaardse wese	[bœeitə·ārdsə vesə]
alien	ruimtewese	[rœeimtə·vesə]
flying saucer	vlieënde skottel	[fliɛndə skottəl]

spaceship	ruimteskip	[rœeimtə·skip]
space station	ruimtestasie	[rœeimtə·stasi]
blast-off	vertrek	[fertrek]

engine	enjin	[ɛndʒin]
nozzle	uitlaatpyp	[œitlāt·pajp]
fuel	brandstof	[brantstof]

cockpit, flight deck	stuurkajuit	[stɪr·kajœit]
antenna	lugdraad	[luχdrāt]
porthole	patryspoort	[patrajs·poərt]
solar panel	sonpaneel	[son·paneəl]
spacesuit	ruimtepak	[rœeimtə·pak]

weightlessness	gewigloosheid	[χeviχloəshæjt]
oxygen	suurstof	[sɪrstof]

docking (in space)	koppeling	[koppeliŋ]
to dock (vi, vt)	koppel	[koppəl]

observatory	observatorium	[observatorium]
telescope	teleskoop	[teleskoəp]
to observe (vt)	waarneem	[vārneəm]
to explore (vt)	eksploreer	[ɛksploreər]

75. The Earth

the Earth	die Aarde	[di ārdə]
the globe (the Earth)	die aardbol	[di ārdbol]
planet	planeet	[planeət]

atmosphere	atmosfeer	[atmosfeər]
geography	geografie	[χeoχrafi]
nature	natuur	[natɪr]

globe (table ~)	aardbol	[ārd·bol]
map	kaart	[kārt]
atlas	atlas	[atlas]

Europe	Europa	[øəropa]
Asia	Asië	[asiɛ]
Africa	Afrika	[afrika]
Australia	Australië	[ɔustraliɛ]
America	Amerika	[amerika]
North America	Noord-Amerika	[noərd-amerika]

South America	**Suid-Amerika**	[sœid-amerika]
Antarctica	**Suidpool**	[sœid·poəl]
the Arctic	**Noordpool**	[noərd·poəl]

76. Cardinal directions

north	**noorde**	[noərdə]
to the north	**na die noorde**	[na di noərdə]
in the north	**in die noorde**	[in di noərdə]
northern (adj)	**noordelik**	[noərdəlik]

south	**suide**	[sœidə]
to the south	**na die suide**	[na di sœidə]
in the south	**in die suide**	[in di sœidə]
southern (adj)	**suidelik**	[sœidəlik]

west	**weste**	[vestə]
to the west	**na die weste**	[na di vestə]
in the west	**in die weste**	[in di vestə]
western (adj)	**westelik**	[vestelik]

east	**ooste**	[oəstə]
to the east	**na die ooste**	[na di oəstə]
in the east	**in die ooste**	[in di oəstə]
eastern (adj)	**oostelik**	[oəstəlik]

77. Sea. Ocean

sea	**see**	[seə]
ocean	**oseaan**	[oseãn]
gulf (bay)	**golf**	[χolf]
straits	**straat**	[strãt]

| land (solid ground) | **land** | [lant] |
| continent (mainland) | **kontinent** | [kontinent] |

island	**eiland**	[æjlant]
peninsula	**skiereiland**	[skir·æjlant]
archipelago	**argipel**	[arχipəl]

bay, cove	**baai**	[bãi]
harbor	**hawe**	[havə]
lagoon	**strandmeer**	[strand·meər]
cape	**kaap**	[kãp]

atoll	**atol**	[atol]
reef	**rif**	[rif]
coral	**koraal**	[korãl]

coral reef	**koraalrif**	[korāl·rif]
deep (adj)	**diep**	[dip]
depth (deep water)	**diepte**	[diptə]
abyss	**afgrond**	[afχront]
trench (e.g., Mariana ~)	**trog**	[troχ]
current (Ocean ~)	**stroming**	[stromiŋ]
to surround (bathe)	**omring**	[omriŋ]
shore	**oewer**	[uvər]
coast	**kus**	[kus]
flow (flood tide)	**hoogwater**	[hoəχ·vatər]
ebb (ebb tide)	**laagwater**	[lāχ·vatər]
shoal	**sandbank**	[sand·bank]
bottom (~ of the sea)	**bodem**	[bodem]
wave	**golf**	[χolf]
crest (~ of a wave)	**kruin**	[krœin]
spume (sea foam)	**skuim**	[skœim]
storm (sea storm)	**storm**	[storm]
hurricane	**orkaan**	[orkān]
tsunami	**tsunami**	[tsunami]
calm (dead ~)	**windstilte**	[vindstiltə]
quiet, calm (adj)	**kalm**	[kalm]
pole	**pool**	[poəl]
polar (adj)	**polêr**	[polær]
latitude	**breedtegraad**	[breedtə·χrāt]
longitude	**lengtegraad**	[leŋtə·χrāt]
parallel	**parallel**	[parallel]
equator	**ewenaar**	[ɛvenār]
sky	**hemel**	[heməl]
horizon	**horison**	[horison]
air	**lug**	[luχ]
lighthouse	**vuurtoring**	[fɪrtoriŋ]
to dive (vi)	**duik**	[dœik]
to sink (ab. boat)	**sink**	[sink]
treasures	**skatte**	[skattə]

78. Seas' and Oceans' names

Atlantic Ocean	**Atlantiese oseaan**	[atlantisə oseān]
Indian Ocean	**Indiese Oseaan**	[indisə oseān]
Pacific Ocean	**Stille Oseaan**	[stillə oseān]
Arctic Ocean	**Noordelike Yssee**	[noərdelikə ajs·see]

Black Sea	**Swart See**	[swart seə]
Red Sea	**Rooi See**	[roj seə]
Yellow Sea	**Geel See**	[χeəl seə]
White Sea	**Witsee**	[vit·seə]

Caspian Sea	**Kaspiese See**	[kaspisə seə]
Dead Sea	**Dooie See**	[doje seə]
Mediterranean Sea	**Middellandse See**	[middəllandsə seə]

| Aegean Sea | **Egeïese See** | [εχejesə seə] |
| Adriatic Sea | **Adriatiese See** | [adriatisə seə] |

Arabian Sea	**Arabiese See**	[arabisə seə]
Sea of Japan	**Japanse See**	[japaŋsə seə]
Bering Sea	**Beringsee**	[beriŋ·seə]
South China Sea	**Suid-Sjinese See**	[sœid-ʃinesə seə]

Coral Sea	**Koraalsee**	[korāl·seə]
Tasman Sea	**Tasmansee**	[tasmaŋ·seə]
Caribbean Sea	**Karibiese See**	[karibisə seə]

| Barents Sea | **Barentssee** | [barents·seə] |
| Kara Sea | **Karasee** | [kara·seə] |

North Sea	**Noordsee**	[noərd·seə]
Baltic Sea	**Baltiese See**	[baltisə seə]
Norwegian Sea	**Noorse See**	[noərsə seə]

79. Mountains

mountain	**berg**	[berχ]
mountain range	**bergreeks**	[berχ·reəks]
mountain ridge	**bergrug**	[berχ·ruχ]

summit, top	**top**	[top]
peak	**piek**	[pik]
foot (~ of the mountain)	**voet**	[fut]
slope (mountainside)	**helling**	[hɛlliŋ]

volcano	**vulkaan**	[fulkān]
active volcano	**aktiewe vulkaan**	[aktivə fulkān]
dormant volcano	**rustende vulkaan**	[rustendə fulkān]

eruption	**uitbarsting**	[œitbarstiŋ]
crater	**krater**	[kratər]
magma	**magma**	[maχma]
lava	**lawa**	[lava]
molten (~ lava)	**gloeiende**	[χlujendə]
canyon	**diepkloof**	[dip·kloəf]
gorge	**kloof**	[kloəf]

| crevice | **skeur** | [skøər] |
| abyss (chasm) | **afgrond** | [afχront] |

pass, col	**bergpas**	[berχ·pas]
plateau	**plato**	[plato]
cliff	**krans**	[kraŋs]
hill	**kop**	[kop]

glacier	**gletser**	[χletsər]
waterfall	**waterval**	[vatər·fal]
geyser	**geiser**	[χæjsər]
lake	**meer**	[meər]

plain	**vlakte**	[flaktə]
landscape	**landskap**	[landskap]
echo	**eggo**	[εχχo]

alpinist	**alpinis**	[alpinis]
rock climber	**bergklimmer**	[berχ·klimmər]
to conquer (in climbing)	**baasraak**	[bãsrãk]
climb (an easy ~)	**beklimming**	[beklimmiŋ]

80. Mountains names

The Alps	**die Alpe**	[di alpə]
Mont Blanc	**Mont Blanc**	[mon blan]
The Pyrenees	**die Pireneë**	[di pirenɛ]

The Carpathians	**die Karpate**	[di karpatə]
The Ural Mountains	**die Oeralgebergte**	[di ural·χəberχtə]
The Caucasus Mountains	**die Koukasus Gebergte**	[di kæʊkasus χəberχtə]
Mount Elbrus	**Elbroes**	[εlbrus]

The Altai Mountains	**die Altai-gebergte**	[di altaj·χəberχtə]
The Tian Shan	**die Tian Shan**	[di tian ʃan]
The Pamir Mountains	**die Pamir**	[di pamir]
The Himalayas	**die Himalajas**	[di himalajas]
Mount Everest	**Everest**	[εverest]

| The Andes | **die Andes** | [di andes] |
| Mount Kilimanjaro | **Kilimanjaro** | [kilimandʒaro] |

81. Rivers

river	**rivier**	[rifir]
spring (natural source)	**bron**	[bron]
riverbed (river channel)	**rivierbed**	[rifir·bet]
basin (river valley)	**stroomgebied**	[stroəm·χebit]

to flow into ...	**uitmond in ...**	[œitmont in ...]
tributary	**syrivier**	[saj·rifir]
bank (of river)	**oewer**	[uvər]
current (stream)	**stroming**	[strominɲ]
downstream (adv)	**stroomafwaarts**	[stroəm·afvārts]
upstream (adv)	**stroomopwaarts**	[stroəm·opvārts]
inundation	**oorstroming**	[oərstrominɲ]
flooding	**oorstroming**	[oərstrominɲ]
to overflow (vi)	**oor sy walle loop**	[oər saj vallə loəp]
to flood (vt)	**oorstroom**	[oərstroəm]
shallow (shoal)	**sandbank**	[sand·bank]
rapids	**stroomversnellings**	[stroəm·fersnɛlliŋs]
dam	**damwal**	[dam·wal]
canal	**kanaal**	[kanāl]
reservoir (artificial lake)	**opgaardam**	[opχār·dam]
sluice, lock	**sluis**	[slœis]
water body (pond, etc.)	**dam**	[dam]
swamp (marshland)	**moeras**	[muras]
bog, marsh	**vlei**	[flæj]
whirlpool	**draaikolk**	[drāj·kolk]
stream (brook)	**spruit**	[sprœit]
drinking (ab. water)	**drink-**	[drink-]
fresh (~ water)	**vars**	[fars]
ice	**ys**	[ajs]
to freeze over	**bevries**	[befris]
(ab. river, etc.)		

82. Rivers' names

Seine	**Seine**	[sæjn]
Loire	**Loire**	[lua:r]
Thames	**Teems**	[tems]
Rhine	**Ryn**	[rajn]
Danube	**Donau**	[donɔu]
Volga	**Wolga**	[volga]
Don	**Don**	[don]
Lena	**Lena**	[lena]
Yellow River	**Geel Rivier**	[χeəl rifir]
Yangtze	**Blou Rivier**	[blæu rifir]
Mekong	**Mekong**	[mekoŋ]

Ganges	**Ganges**	[xaŋəs]
Nile River	**Nyl**	[najl]
Congo River	**Kongorivier**	[kongo·rifir]
Okavango River	**Okavango**	[okavango]
Zambezi River	**Zambezi**	[sambesi]
Limpopo River	**Limpopo**	[limpopo]
Mississippi River	**Mississippi**	[mississippi]

83. Forest

forest, wood	**bos**	[bos]
forest (as adj)	**bos-**	[bos-]
thick forest	**woud**	[væʊt]
grove	**boord**	[boərt]
forest clearing	**oopte**	[oəptə]
thicket	**struikgewas**	[strœik·xevas]
scrubland	**struikveld**	[strœik·fɛlt]
footpath (troddenpath)	**paadjie**	[pãdʒi]
gully	**donga**	[donχa]
tree	**boom**	[boəm]
leaf	**blaar**	[blãr]
leaves (foliage)	**blare**	[blarə]
fall of leaves	**val van die blare**	[fal fan di blarə]
to fall (ab. leaves)	**val**	[fal]
top (of the tree)	**boomtop**	[boəm·top]
branch	**tak**	[tak]
bough	**tak**	[tak]
bud (on shrub, tree)	**knop**	[knop]
needle (of pine tree)	**naald**	[nãlt]
pine cone	**dennebol**	[dɛnnə·bol]
hollow (in a tree)	**holte**	[holtə]
nest	**nes**	[nes]
burrow (animal hole)	**gat**	[χat]
trunk	**stam**	[stam]
root	**wortel**	[vortəl]
bark	**bas**	[bas]
moss	**mos**	[mos]
to uproot (remove trees or tree stumps)	**ontwortel**	[ontwortəl]
to chop down	**omkap**	[omkap]
to deforest (vt)	**ontbos**	[ontbos]

tree stump	**boomstomp**	[boəm·stomp]
campfire	**kampvuur**	[kampfɪr]
forest fire	**bosbrand**	[bos·brant]
to extinguish (vt)	**blus**	[blus]

forest ranger	**boswagter**	[bos·waχtər]
protection	**beskerming**	[beskermiŋ]
to protect (~ nature)	**beskerm**	[beskerm]
poacher	**wildstroper**	[vilt·stropər]
steel trap	**slagyster**	[slaχ·ajstər]

| to gather, to pick (vt) | **pluk** | [pluk] |
| to lose one's way | **verdwaal** | [ferdwāl] |

84. Natural resources

natural resources	**natuurlike bronne**	[natɪrlikə bronnə]
minerals	**minerale**	[mineralə]
deposits	**lae**	[laə]
field (e.g., oilfield)	**veld**	[fɛlt]

to mine (extract)	**myn**	[majn]
mining (extraction)	**myn**	[majn]
ore	**erts**	[ɛrts]
mine (e.g., for coal)	**myn**	[majn]
shaft (mine ~)	**mynskag**	[majn·skaχ]
miner	**mynwerker**	[majn·werkər]

| gas (natural ~) | **gas** | [χas] |
| gas pipeline | **gaspyp** | [χas·pajp] |

oil (petroleum)	**olie**	[oli]
oil pipeline	**olipypleiding**	[oli·pajp·læjdiŋ]
oil well	**oliebron**	[oli·bron]
derrick (tower)	**boortoring**	[boər·toriŋ]
tanker	**tenkskip**	[tɛnk·skip]

sand	**sand**	[sant]
limestone	**kalksteen**	[kalksteən]
gravel	**gruis**	[χrœis]
peat	**veengrond**	[feənχront]
clay	**klei**	[klæj]
coal	**steenkool**	[steən·koəl]

iron (ore)	**yster**	[ajstər]
gold	**goud**	[χæʊt]
silver	**silwer**	[silwər]
nickel	**nikkel**	[nikkəl]
copper	**koper**	[kopər]
zinc	**sink**	[sink]

manganese	mangaan	[manχān]
mercury	kwik	[kwik]
lead	lood	[loət]

mineral	mineraal	[minerāl]
crystal	kristal	[kristal]
marble	marmer	[marmər]
uranium	uraan	[urān]

85. Weather

weather	weer	[veər]
weather forecast	weersvoorspelling	[veərs·foərspɛliŋ]
temperature	temperatuur	[temperatɪr]
thermometer	termometer	[termometər]
barometer	barometer	[barometər]

| humid (adj) | klam | [klam] |
| humidity | vogtigheid | [foχtiχæjt] |

heat (extreme ~)	hitte	[hittə]
hot (torrid)	heet	[heət]
it's hot	dis vrekwarm	[dis frekvarm]

| it's warm | dit is warm | [dit is varm] |
| warm (moderately hot) | louwarm | [læʊvarm] |

| it's cold | dis koud | [dis kæʊt] |
| cold (adj) | koud | [kæʊt] |

sun	son	[son]
to shine (vi)	skyn	[skajn]
sunny (day)	sonnig	[sonnəχ]
to come up (vi)	opkom	[opkom]
to set (vi)	ondergaan	[ondərχān]

cloud	wolk	[volk]
cloudy (adj)	bewolk	[bevolk]
rain cloud	reënwolk	[reɛn·wolk]
somber (gloomy)	somber	[sombər]

rain	reën	[reɛn]
it's raining	dit reën	[dit reɛn]
rainy (~ day, weather)	reënerig	[reɛnerəχ]
to drizzle (vi)	motreën	[motreɛn]

pouring rain	stortbui	[stortbœi]
downpour	reënvlaag	[reɛn·flāχ]
heavy (e.g., ~ rain)	swaar	[swār]
puddle	poeletjie	[puləki]

to get wet (in rain)	**nat word**	[nat vort]
fog (mist)	**mis**	[mis]
foggy	**mistig**	[mistəχ]
snow	**sneeu**	[sniʊ]
it's snowing	**dit sneeu**	[dit sniʊ]

86. Severe weather. Natural disasters

thunderstorm	**donderstorm**	[dondər·storm]
lightning (~ strike)	**weerlig**	[veərləχ]
to flash (vi)	**flits**	[flits]
thunder	**donder**	[dondər]
to thunder (vi)	**donder**	[dondər]
it's thundering	**dit donder**	[dit dondər]
hail	**hael**	[haəl]
it's hailing	**dit hael**	[dit haəl]
to flood (vt)	**oorstroom**	[oərstroəm]
flood, inundation	**oorstroming**	[oərstromiŋ]
earthquake	**aardbewing**	[ārd·beviŋ]
tremor, quake	**aardskok**	[ārd·skok]
epicenter	**episentrum**	[ɛpisentrum]
eruption	**uitbarsting**	[œitbarstiŋ]
lava	**lawa**	[lava]
twister, tornado	**tornado**	[tornado]
typhoon	**tifoon**	[tifoən]
hurricane	**orkaan**	[orkān]
storm	**storm**	[storm]
tsunami	**tsunami**	[tsunami]
cyclone	**sikloon**	[sikloən]
bad weather	**slegte weer**	[sleχtə veər]
fire (accident)	**brand**	[brant]
disaster	**ramp**	[ramp]
meteorite	**meteoriet**	[meteorit]
avalanche	**lawine**	[lavinə]
snowslide	**sneeulawine**	[sniʊ·lavinə]
blizzard	**sneeustorm**	[sniʊ·storm]
snowstorm	**sneeustorm**	[sniʊ·storm]

FAUNA

87. Mammals. Predators

predator	**roofdier**	[roef·dir]
tiger	**tier**	[tir]
lion	**leeu**	[liʊ]
wolf	**wolf**	[volf]
fox	**vos**	[fos]
jaguar	**jaguar**	[jaχuar]
leopard	**luiperd**	[lœipert]
cheetah	**jagluiperd**	[jaχ·lœipert]
black panther	**swart luiperd**	[swart lœipert]
puma	**poema**	[puma]
snow leopard	**sneeuluiperd**	[sniʊ·lœipert]
lynx	**los**	[los]
coyote	**prèriewolf**	[præri·volf]
jackal	**jakkals**	[jakkals]
hyena	**hiëna**	[hiɛna]

88. Wild animals

animal	**dier**	[dir]
beast (animal)	**beest**	[beəst]
squirrel	**eekhoring**	[eəkhoriŋ]
hedgehog	**krimpvarkie**	[krimpfarki]
hare	**hasie**	[hasi]
rabbit	**konyn**	[konajn]
badger	**das**	[das]
raccoon	**wasbeer**	[vasbeər]
hamster	**hamster**	[hamstər]
marmot	**marmot**	[marmot]
mole	**mol**	[mol]
mouse	**muis**	[mœis]
rat	**rot**	[rot]
bat	**vlermuis**	[fler·mœis]
ermine	**hermelyn**	[herməlajn]
sable	**sabel, sabeldier**	[sabəl], [sabəl·dir]

marten	**marter**	[martər]
weasel	**wesel**	[vesəl]
mink	**nerts**	[nerts]
beaver	**bewer**	[bevər]
otter	**otter**	[ottər]
horse	**perd**	[pert]
moose	**eland**	[ɕlant]
deer	**hert**	[hert]
camel	**kameel**	[kameəl]
bison	**bison**	[bison]
aurochs	**wisent**	[visent]
buffalo	**buffel**	[buffəl]
zebra	**sebra, kwagga**	[sebra], [kwaχχa]
antelope	**wildsbok**	[vilds·bok]
roe deer	**reebok**	[reəbok]
fallow deer	**damhert**	[damhert]
chamois	**gems**	[χems]
wild boar	**wildevark**	[vildə·fark]
whale	**walvis**	[valfis]
seal	**seehond**	[seə·hont]
walrus	**walrus**	[valrus]
fur seal	**seebeer**	[seə·beər]
dolphin	**dolfyn**	[dolfajn]
bear	**beer**	[beər]
polar bear	**ysbeer**	[ajs·beər]
panda	**panda**	[panda]
monkey	**aap**	[āp]
chimpanzee	**sjimpansee**	[ʃimpaŋseə]
orangutan	**orangoetang**	[oranχutaŋ]
gorilla	**gorilla**	[χorilla]
macaque	**makaak**	[makāk]
gibbon	**gibbon**	[χibbon]
elephant	**olifant**	[olifant]
rhinoceros	**renoster**	[renostər]
giraffe	**kameelperd**	[kameəl·pert]
hippopotamus	**seekoei**	[seə·kui]
kangaroo	**kangaroe**	[kanχaru]
koala (bear)	**koala**	[koala]
mongoose	**muishond**	[mœis·hont]
chinchilla	**chinchilla, tjintjilla**	[tʃin·tʃila]
skunk	**stinkmuishond**	[stinkmœis·hont]
porcupine	**ystervark**	[ajstər·fark]

89. Domestic animals

cat	kat	[kat]
tomcat	kater	[katər]
dog	hond	[hont]

horse	perd	[pert]
stallion (male horse)	hings	[hiŋs]
mare	merrie	[merri]

cow	koei	[kui]
bull	bul	[bul]
ox	os	[os]

sheep (ewe)	skaap	[skāp]
ram	ram	[ram]
goat	bok	[bok]
billy goat, he-goat	bokram	[bok·ram]

| donkey | donkie, esel | [donki], [eisəl] |
| mule | muil | [mœil] |

pig, hog	vark	[fark]
piglet	varkie	[farki]
rabbit	konyn	[konajn]

| hen (chicken) | hoender, hen | [hundər], [hen] |
| rooster | haan | [hān] |

duck	eend	[eent]
drake	mannetjieseend	[mannəkis·eent]
goose	gans	[χaŋs]

| tom turkey, gobbler | kalkoenmannetjie | [kalkun·mannəki] |
| turkey (hen) | kalkoen | [kalkun] |

domestic animals	huisdiere	[hœis·dirə]
tame (e.g., ~ hamster)	mak	[mak]
to tame (vt)	mak maak	[mak māk]
to breed (vt)	teel	[teəl]

farm	plaas	[plās]
poultry	pluimvee	[plœimfeə]
cattle	beeste	[beəstə]
herd (cattle)	kudde	[kuddə]

stable	stal	[stal]
pigpen	varkstal	[fark·stal]
cowshed	koeistal	[kui·stal]
rabbit hutch	konynehok	[konajnə·hok]
hen house	hoenderhok	[hundər·hok]

90. Birds

bird	**voël**	[foɛl]
pigeon	**duif**	[dœif]
sparrow	**mossie**	[mossi]
tit (great tit)	**mees**	[meəs]
magpie	**ekster**	[ɛkstər]
raven	**raaf**	[rãf]
crow	**kraai**	[krãi]
jackdaw	**kerkkraai**	[kerk·krãi]
rook	**roek**	[ruk]
duck	**eend**	[eent]
goose	**gans**	[χaŋs]
pheasant	**fisant**	[fisant]
eagle	**arend**	[arɛnt]
hawk	**sperwer**	[sperwər]
falcon	**valk**	[falk]
vulture	**aasvoël**	[ãsfoɛl]
condor (Andean ~)	**kondor**	[kondor]
swan	**swaan**	[swãn]
crane	**kraanvoël**	[krãn·foɛl]
stork	**ooievaar**	[ojefãr]
parrot	**papegaai**	[papəχãi]
hummingbird	**kolibrie**	[kolibri]
peacock	**pou**	[pæʊ]
ostrich	**volstruis**	[folstrœis]
heron	**reier**	[ræjer]
flamingo	**flamink**	[flamink]
pelican	**pelikaan**	[pelikãn]
nightingale	**nagtegaal**	[naχteχãl]
swallow	**swael**	[swaəl]
thrush	**lyster**	[lajstər]
song thrush	**sanglyster**	[saŋlajstər]
blackbird	**merel**	[merəl]
swift	**windswael**	[vindswaəl]
lark	**lewerik**	[leverik]
quail	**kwartel**	[kwartəl]
woodpecker	**speg**	[speχ]
cuckoo	**koekoek**	[kukuk]
owl	**uil**	[œil]
eagle owl	**ooruil**	[oərœil]

wood grouse	**auerhoen**	[ɔuer·hun]
black grouse	**korhoen**	[korhun]
partridge	**patrys**	[patrajs]
starling	**spreeu**	[spriʊ]
canary	**kanarie**	[kanari]
hazel grouse	**bonasa hoen**	[bonasa hun]
chaffinch	**gryskoppie**	[χrajskoppi]
bullfinch	**bloedvink**	[bludfink]
seagull	**seemeeu**	[seəmiʊ]
albatross	**albatros**	[albatros]
penguin	**pikkewyn**	[pikkəvajn]

91. Fish. Marine animals

bream	**brasem**	[brasem]
carp	**karp**	[karp]
perch	**baars**	[bārs]
catfish	**katvis, seebaber**	[katfis], [see·babər]
pike	**snoek**	[snuk]
salmon	**salm**	[salm]
sturgeon	**steur**	[støər]
herring	**haring**	[hariŋ]
Atlantic salmon	**atlantiese salm**	[atlantisə salm]
mackerel	**makriel**	[makril]
flatfish	**platvis**	[platfis]
zander, pike perch	**varswatersnoek**	[farswatər·snuk]
cod	**kabeljou**	[kabeljæʊ]
tuna	**tuna**	[tuna]
trout	**forel**	[forəl]
eel	**paling**	[paliŋ]
electric ray	**drilvis**	[drilfis]
moray eel	**bontpaling**	[bontpaliŋ]
piranha	**piranha**	[piranha]
shark	**haai**	[hāi]
dolphin	**dolfyn**	[dolfajn]
whale	**walvis**	[valfis]
crab	**krap**	[krap]
jellyfish	**jellievis**	[jelli·fis]
octopus	**seekat**	[see·kat]
starfish	**seester**	[see·stər]
sea urchin	**see-egel, seekastaiing**	[see-eχel], [see·kastajiŋ]

seahorse	**seeperdjie**	[see·perdʒi]
oyster	**oester**	[ustər]
shrimp	**garnaal**	[χarnāl]
lobster	**kreef**	[kreəf]
spiny lobster	**seekreef**	[see·kreəf]

92. Amphibians. Reptiles

| snake | **slang** | [slaŋ] |
| venomous (snake) | **giftig** | [χiftəχ] |

viper	**adder**	[addər]
cobra	**kobra**	[kobra]
python	**luislang**	[lœislaŋ]
boa	**boa, konstriktorslang**	[boa], [kɔŋstriktor·slaŋ]

grass snake	**ringslang**	[riŋ·slaŋ]
rattle snake	**ratelslang**	[ratəl·slaŋ]
anaconda	**anakonda**	[anakonda]

lizard	**akkedis**	[akkedis]
iguana	**leguaan**	[leχuān]
monitor lizard	**likkewaan**	[likkevān]
salamander	**salamander**	[salamandər]
chameleon	**verkleurmannetjie**	[ferkløer·manneki]
scorpion	**skerpioen**	[skerpiun]

turtle	**skilpad**	[skilpat]
frog	**padda**	[padda]
toad	**brulpadda**	[brul·padda]
crocodile	**krokodil**	[krokodil]

93. Insects

insect, bug	**insek**	[insek]
butterfly	**skoenlapper**	[skunlappər]
ant	**mier**	[mir]
fly	**vlieg**	[fliχ]
mosquito	**muskiet**	[muskit]
beetle	**kewer**	[kevər]

wasp	**perdeby**	[perdə·baj]
bee	**by**	[baj]
bumblebee	**hommelby**	[homməl·baj]
gadfly (botfly)	**perdevlieg**	[perdə·fliχ]

| spider | **spinnekop** | [spinnə·kop] |
| spiderweb | **spinnerak** | [spinnə·rak] |

dragonfly	naaldekoker	[nãldə·kokər]
grasshopper	sprinkaan	[sprinkãn]
moth (night butterfly)	mot	[mot]

cockroach	kakkerlak	[kakkerlak]
tick	bosluis	[boslœis]
flea	vlooi	[floj]
midge	muggie	[muχχi]

locust	treksprinkhaan	[trek·sprinkhãn]
snail	slak	[slak]
cricket	kriek	[krik]
lightning bug	vuurvliegie	[fɪrfliχi]
ladybug	lieweheersbesie	[liveheərs·besi]
cockchafer	lentekewer	[lentekevər]

leech	bloedsuier	[blud·sœiər]
caterpillar	ruspe	[ruspə]
earthworm	erdwurm	[ɛrd·vurm]
larva	larwe	[larvə]

FLORA

94. Trees

tree	**boom**	[boəm]
deciduous (adj)	**bladwisselend**	[bladwisselent]
coniferous (adj)	**kegeldraend**	[keχεldraent]
evergreen (adj)	**immergroen**	[immərχrun]
apple tree	**appelboom**	[appɛl·boəm]
pear tree	**peerboom**	[peər·boəm]
cherry tree	**kersieboom**	[kersi·boəm]
sweet cherry tree	**soetkersieboom**	[sutkersi·boəm]
sour cherry tree	**suurkersieboom**	[sɪrkersi·boəm]
plum tree	**pruimeboom**	[prœimə·boəm]
birch	**berk**	[berk]
oak	**eik**	[æjk]
linden tree	**lindeboom**	[lində·boəm]
aspen	**trilpopulier**	[trilpopulir]
maple	**esdoring**	[ɛsdoriŋ]
spruce	**spar**	[spar]
pine	**denneboom**	[dɛnnə·boəm]
larch	**lorkeboom**	[lorkə·boəm]
fir tree	**den**	[den]
cedar	**seder**	[sedər]
poplar	**populier**	[populir]
rowan	**lysterbessie**	[lajstərbɛssi]
willow	**wilger**	[vilχər]
alder	**els**	[ɛls]
beech	**beuk**	[bøək]
elm	**olm**	[olm]
ash (tree)	**esboom**	[ɛs·boəm]
chestnut	**kastaiing**	[kastajiŋ]
magnolia	**magnolia**	[maχnolia]
palm tree	**palm**	[palm]
cypress	**sipres**	[sipres]
mangrove	**wortelboom**	[vortəl·boəm]
baobab	**kremetart**	[kremetart]
eucalyptus	**bloekom**	[blukom]
sequoia	**mammoetboom**	[mammut·boəm]

95. Shrubs

bush	**struik**	[strœik]
shrub	**bossie**	[bossi]
grapevine	**wingerdstok**	[viŋərd·stok]
vineyard	**wingerd**	[viŋərt]
raspberry bush	**framboosstruik**	[framboəs·strœik]
blackcurrant bush	**swartbessiestruik**	[swartbɛssi·strœik]
redcurrant bush	**rooi aalbessiestruik**	[roj ãlbɛssi·strœik]
gooseberry bush	**appelliefiestruik**	[appɛllifi·strœik]
acacia	**akasia**	[akasia]
barberry	**suurbessie**	[sɪr·bɛssi]
jasmine	**jasmyn**	[jasmajn]
juniper	**jenewer**	[jenevər]
rosebush	**roosstruik**	[roəs·strœik]
dog rose	**hondsroos**	[honds·roəs]

96. Fruits. Berries

fruit	**vrug**	[fruχ]
fruits	**vrugte**	[fruχtə]
apple	**appel**	[appəl]
pear	**peer**	[peər]
plum	**pruim**	[prœim]
strawberry (garden ~)	**aarbei**	[ãrbæj]
cherry	**kersie**	[kersi]
sour cherry	**suurkersie**	[sɪr·kersi]
sweet cherry	**soetkersie**	[sut·kersi]
grape	**druif**	[drœif]
raspberry	**framboos**	[framboəs]
blackcurrant	**swartbessie**	[swartbɛssi]
redcurrant	**rooi aalbessie**	[roj ãlbɛssi]
gooseberry	**appelliefie**	[appɛllifi]
cranberry	**bosbessie**	[bosbɛssi]
orange	**lemoen**	[lemun]
mandarin	**nartjie**	[narki]
pineapple	**pynappel**	[pajnappəl]
banana	**piesang**	[pisaŋ]
date	**dadel**	[dadəl]
lemon	**suurlemoen**	[sɪr·lemun]
apricot	**appelkoos**	[appɛlkoəs]

peach	perske	[perskə]
kiwi	kiwi, kiwivrug	[kivi], [kivi·fruχ]
grapefruit	pomelo	[pomelo]

berry	bessie	[bɛssi]
berries	bessies	[bɛssis]
cowberry	pryselbessie	[prajsɛlbɛssi]
wild strawberry	wilde aarbei	[vildə ārbæj]
bilberry	bloubessie	[blæʊbɛssi]

97. Flowers. Plants

| flower | blom | [blom] |
| bouquet (of flowers) | boeket | [buket] |

rose (flower)	roos	[roəs]
tulip	tulp	[tulp]
carnation	angelier	[anχəlir]
gladiolus	swaardlelie	[swārd·leli]

cornflower	koringblom	[koriŋblom]
harebell	grasklokkie	[χras·klokki]
dandelion	perdeblom	[perdə·blom]
camomile	kamille	[kamillə]

aloe	aalwyn	[ālwajn]
cactus	kaktus	[kaktus]
rubber plant, ficus	rubberplant	[rubbər·plant]

lily	lelie	[leli]
geranium	malva	[malfa]
hyacinth	hiasint	[hiasint]

mimosa	mimosa	[mimosa]
narcissus	narsing	[narsiŋ]
nasturtium	kappertjie	[kapperki]

orchid	orgidee	[orχideə]
peony	pinksterroos	[pinkstər·roəs]
violet	viooltjie	[fioəlki]

pansy	gesiggie	[χesiχi]
forget-me-not	vergeet-my-nietjie	[ferχeət-maj-niki]
daisy	madeliefie	[madelifi]

poppy	papawer	[papavər]
hemp	hennep	[hɛnnəp]
mint	kruisement	[krœisəment]
lily of the valley	dallelie	[dalleli]
snowdrop	sneeuklokkie	[sniʊ·klokki]

nettle	**brandnetel**	[brant·netəl]
sorrel	**veldsuring**	[fɛltsuriŋ]
water lily	**waterlelie**	[vatər·leli]
fern	**varing**	[fariŋ]
lichen	**korsmos**	[korsmos]

greenhouse (tropical ~)	**broeikas**	[bruikas]
lawn	**grasperk**	[χras·perk]
flowerbed	**blombed**	[blom·bet]

plant	**plant**	[plant]
grass	**gras**	[χras]
blade of grass	**grasspriet**	[χras·sprit]

leaf	**blaar**	[blãr]
petal	**kroonblaar**	[kroen·blãr]
stem	**stingel**	[stiŋəl]
tuber	**knol**	[knol]

| young plant (shoot) | **saailing** | [sãjliŋ] |
| thorn | **doring** | [doriŋ] |

to blossom (vi)	**bloei**	[blui]
to fade, to wither	**verlep**	[ferlep]
smell (odor)	**reuk**	[røək]
to cut (flowers)	**sny**	[snaj]
to pick (a flower)	**pluk**	[pluk]

98. Cereals, grains

grain	**graan**	[χrãn]
cereal crops	**graangewasse**	[χrãn·χəwassə]
ear (of barley, etc.)	**aar**	[ãr]

wheat	**koring**	[koriŋ]
rye	**rog**	[roχ]
oats	**hawer**	[havər]

| millet | **gierst** | [χirst] |
| barley | **gars** | [χars] |

corn	**mielie**	[mili]
rice	**rys**	[rajs]
buckwheat	**bokwiet**	[bokwit]

pea plant	**ertjie**	[ɛrki]
kidney bean	**nierboon**	[nir·boən]
soy	**soja**	[soja]
lentil	**lensie**	[lɛnsi]
beans (pulse crops)	**boontjies**	[boənkis]

COUNTRIES OF THE WORLD

99. Countries. Part 1

Afghanistan	**Afghanistan**	[afχanistan]
Albania	**Albanië**	[albaniɛ]
Argentina	**Argentinië**	[arχentiniɛ]
Armenia	**Armenië**	[armeniɛ]
Australia	**Australië**	[ɔustraliɛ]
Austria	**Oostenryk**	[oəstenrajk]
Azerbaijan	**Azerbeidjan**	[azerbæjdjan]
The Bahamas	**die Bahamas**	[di bahamas]
Bangladesh	**Bangladesj**	[bangladeʃ]
Belarus	**Belarus**	[belarus]
Belgium	**België**	[belχiɛ]
Bolivia	**Bolivië**	[boliviɛ]
Bosnia and Herzegovina	**Bosnië & Herzegowina**	[bosniɛ en hersegovina]
Brazil	**Brasilië**	[brasiliɛ]
Bulgaria	**Bulgarye**	[bulχaraje]
Cambodia	**Kambodja**	[kambodja]
Canada	**Kanada**	[kanada]
Chile	**Chili**	[tʃili]
China	**Sjina**	[ʃina]
Colombia	**Colombia, Kolombië**	[kolombia], [kolombiɛ]
Croatia	**Kroasië**	[kroasiɛ]
Cuba	**Kuba**	[kuba]
Cyprus	**Ciprus**	[siprus]
Czech Republic	**Tjeggië**	[tʃeχiɛ]
Denmark	**Denemarke**	[denemarkə]
Dominican Republic	**Dominikaanse Republiek**	[dominikãŋsə republik]
Ecuador	**Ecuador**	[ɛkuador]
Egypt	**Egipte**	[ɛχiptə]
England	**Engeland**	[ɛŋəlant]
Estonia	**Estland**	[ɛstlant]
Finland	**Finland**	[finlant]
France	**Frankryk**	[frankrajk]
French Polynesia	**Frans-Polinesië**	[fraŋs-polinesiɛ]
Georgia	**Georgië**	[χeorχiɛ]
Germany	**Duitsland**	[dœitslant]
Ghana	**Ghana**	[χana]
Great Britain	**Groot-Brittanje**	[χroət-brittanje]
Greece	**Griekeland**	[χrikəlant]

| Haiti | **Haïti** | [haïti] |
| Hungary | **Hongarye** | [honχaraje] |

100. Countries. Part 2

Iceland	**Ysland**	[ajslant]
India	**Indië**	[indiɛ]
Indonesia	**Indonesië**	[indonesiɛ]
Iran	**Iran**	[iran]
Iraq	**Irak**	[irak]
Ireland	**Ierland**	[irlant]
Israel	**Israel**	[israəl]
Italy	**Italië**	[italiɛ]

Jamaica	**Jamaika**	[jamajka]
Japan	**Japan**	[japan]
Jordan	**Jordanië**	[jordaniɛ]
Kazakhstan	**Kazakstan**	[kasakstan]
Kenya	**Kenia**	[kenia]
Kirghizia	**Kirgisië**	[kirχisiɛ]
Kuwait	**Kuwait**	[kuvajt]

Laos	**Laos**	[laos]
Latvia	**Letland**	[letlant]
Lebanon	**Libanon**	[libanon]
Libya	**Libië**	[libiɛ]
Liechtenstein	**Lichtenstein**	[liχtɛŋstejn]
Lithuania	**Litoue**	[litæʊə]
Luxembourg	**Luksemburg**	[luksemburχ]

Macedonia (Republic of ~)	**Masedonië**	[masedoniɛ]
Madagascar	**Madagaskar**	[madaχaskar]
Malaysia	**Maleisië**	[malæjsiɛ]
Malta	**Malta**	[malta]
Mexico	**Meksiko**	[meksiko]
Moldova, Moldavia	**Moldawië**	[moldaviɛ]

Monaco	**Monako**	[monako]
Mongolia	**Mongolië**	[monχoliɛ]
Montenegro	**Montenegro**	[montənegro]

| Morocco | **Marokko** | [marokko] |
| Myanmar | **Myanmar** | [mjanmar] |

Namibia	**Namibië**	[namibiɛ]
Nepal	**Nepal**	[nepal]
Netherlands	**Nederland**	[nedərlant]
New Zealand	**Nieu-Seeland**	[niu-seəlant]
North Korea	**Noord-Korea**	[noərd-korea]
Norway	**Noorweë**	[noərweɛ]

101. Countries. Part 3

Pakistan	**Pakistan**	[pakistan]
Palestine	**Palestina**	[palestina]
Panama	**Panama**	[panama]
Paraguay	**Paraguay**	[paragwaj]
Peru	**Peru**	[peru]
Poland	**Pole**	[polə]
Portugal	**Portugal**	[portuχal]
Romania	**Roemenië**	[rumeniɛ]
Russia	**Rusland**	[ruslant]
Saudi Arabia	**Saoedi-Arabië**	[saudi-arabiɛ]
Scotland	**Skotland**	[skotlant]
Senegal	**Senegal**	[seneχal]
Serbia	**Serwië**	[serwiɛ]
Slovakia	**Slowakye**	[slovakajə]
Slovenia	**Slovenië**	[slofeniɛ]
South Africa	**Suid-Afrika**	[sœid-afrika]
South Korea	**Suid-Korea**	[sœid-korea]
Spain	**Spanje**	[spanjə]
Suriname	**Suriname**	[surinamə]
Sweden	**Swede**	[swedə]
Switzerland	**Switserland**	[switsərlant]
Syria	**Sirië**	[siriɛ]
Taiwan	**Taiwan**	[tajvan]
Tajikistan	**Tadjikistan**	[tadʒikistan]
Tanzania	**Tanzanië**	[tansaniɛ]
Tasmania	**Tasmanië**	[tasmaniɛ]
Thailand	**Thailand**	[tajlant]
Tunisia	**Tunisië**	[tunisiɛ]
Turkey	**Turkye**	[turkajə]
Turkmenistan	**Turkmenistan**	[turkmenistan]
Ukraine	**Oekraïne**	[ukraïnə]
United Arab Emirates	**Verenigde Arabiese Emirate**	[fereniχdə arabisə emiratə]
United States of America	**Verenigde State van Amerika**	[fereniχdə statə fan amerika]
Uruguay	**Uruguay**	[urugwaj]
Uzbekistan	**Oezbekistan**	[uzbekistan]
Vatican	**Vatikaan**	[fatikān]
Venezuela	**Venezuela**	[fenesuela]
Vietnam	**Viëtnam**	[viɛtnam]
Zanzibar	**Zanzibar**	[zanzibar]

www.ingramcontent.com/pod-product-compliance
Lightning Source LLC
Chambersburg PA
CBHW070815050426
42452CB00011B/2055